The Gay and Lesbian Psychotherapy Treatment Planner

Practice *Planners*™ Series

Treatment *Planners*

The Chemical Dependence Treatment Planner
The Continuum of Care Treatment Planner
The Couples Psychotherapy Treatment Planner
The Employee Assistance Treatment Planner
The Pastoral Counseling Treatment Planner
The Older Adult Psychotherapy Treatment Planner
The Complete Adult Psychotherapy Treatment Planner, 2e
The Behavioral Medicine Treatment Planner
The Group Therapy Treatment Planner
The Gay and Lesbian Psychotherapy Treatment Planner
The Child Psychotherapy Treatment Planner, 2e
The Adolescent Psychotherapy Treatment Planner, 2e
The Family Psychotherapy Treatment Planner
The Persistent Mental Illness Treatment Planner
The Mental Retardation and Developmental Disability Treatment Planner
The Neuropsychological Treatment Planner
The Social Work and Human Services Treatment Planner

Homework *Planners*

Brief Therapy Homework Planner
Brief Couples Therapy Homework Planner
Chemical Dependence Treatment Homework Planner
Brief Child Therapy Homework Planner
Brief Adolescent Therapy Homework Planner
Employee Assistance Homework Planner

Documentation *Sourcebooks*

The Clinical Documentation Sourcebook
The Forensic Documentation Sourcebook
The Psychotherapy Documentation Primer
The Chemical Dependence Treatment Documentation Sourcebook
The Clinical Child Documentation Sourcebook
The Couple and Family Clinical Documentation Sourcebook
The Clinical Documentation Sourcebook, 2e
The Continuum of Care Clinical Documentation Sourcebook

Presentation *Planners*

The Couples and Family Presentation Planner
The Life Skills Presentation Planner
The Work Skills Presentation Planner

Progress Notes *Planners*

The Adult Psychotherapy Progress Notes Planner
The Child Psychotherapy Progress Notes Planner
The Adolescent Psychotherapy Progress Notes Planner

The Gay and Lesbian Psychotherapy Treatment Planner

J.M. Evosevich

Michael Avriette

JOHN WILEY & SONS, INC.

New York • Chichester • Weinheim • Brisbane • Singapore • Toronto

Published by John Wiley & Sons, Inc.

Published simultaneously in Canada.

This publication is designed to provide accurate and authoritative information in regard to the subject matter covered. It is sold with the understanding that the publisher is not engaged in rendering professional services. If legal, accounting, medical, psychological or any other expert assistance is required, the services of a competent professional person should be sought.

Designations used by companies to distinguish their products are often claimed as trademarks. In all instances where John Wiley & Sons, Inc. is aware of a claim, the product names appear in initial capital or all capital letters. Readers, however, should contact the appropriate companies for more complete information regarding trademarks and registration.

Library of Congress Cataloging-in-Publication Data:

Evosevich, J.M.
    The gay and lesbian psychotherapy treatment planner / J.M.
Evosevich and Michael Avriette.
        p.   cm. — (Practice planners series)
    ISBN 0-471-35080-X (paper : alk. paper). — ISBN 0-471-35081-8
(paper/disk : alk. paper)
    1. Gay—Mental health.   2. Lesbians—Mental health.
3. Psychotherapy.   4. Psychotherapist and patient.   I. Avriette,
Michael.   II. Title.   III. Series: Practice planners.
    RC558.E96   1999
    616.89′14′08664—dc21   99-38821

Printed in the United States of America.

10   9   8   7   6   5   4   3   2   1

CONTENTS

PREFACE

The authors' primary purpose in writing *The Gay and Lesbian Psychotherapy Treatment Planner* was to assist mental health professionals in organizing and documenting their psychotherapeutic services to homosexual men and women. At the time of this writing, no other book or manual has been written to assist therapists in this process. The need is great. Managed care companies are demanding more in less time and lesbian women and gay men expect and deserve treatment that includes their special needs.

Ideally, psychotherapy addresses the whole person, including one's interactions with the greater culture and the impact that has on psychosocial functioning. This is particularly important with marginalized groups. Sexual orientation has a profound impact upon this interaction. Lesbians and gay men are born into and socialized in a homophobic society. They encounter homophobia not only as an external stressor, but as an internal set of beliefs. In other words, society devalues homosexuals and often homosexuals devalue themselves. This dual process affects peoples' ability to resolve conflicts in their lives. Consequently, we have included objectives of addressing internalized homophobia in nearly every problem in this *Planner*. This is but one example of how treatment with lesbians and gay men requires special consideration.

There is not a single path to treatment success. Nor is it necessary for the therapist to be gay/lesbian. This book is the product of collaboration between two openly gay therapists, and one heterosexual series editor. We believe the book is richer and more balanced because of this. The authors have had to challenge their assumptions, face their biases, and recognize different perspectives; not unlike the treatment process itself.

We would like to thank our editor at John Wiley and Sons, Kelly Franklin, for all her support from the first e-mail suggesting this project to the final submission. We also like to thank our individual families for their support (David Cantwell, Joshua Cantwell Evosevich, Gene and Margaret Avriette, and Judy Jongsma). Though writing the book was a pleasure, it took time away from the ones we love and sometimes tried their patience. Thank you. Finally, we would like to thank the many lesbians and gay men with whom we have worked over the years. Without them, this book could not have been written.

J. M. Evosevich
Michael Avriette
Arthur E. Jongsma, Jr., Series Editor

INTRODUCTION

The relationship between the mental health professions and lesbians and gay men has changed dramatically in the last quarter of this century. Prior to the 1970s, the goal of treatment was to change homosexuals into heterosexuals, with disastrous results. Psychoanalysis, castration, hormone therapy, and insulin shock were the "options" available to gay men and lesbians seeking help. This changed in the early 1970s as lesbian and gay activists challenged the notion that homosexuality was a sickness. Their efforts were supported when the American Psychiatric Association decided to remove homosexuality from the *DSM* in 1973. It took another decade to remove the category "ego-dystonic" homosexuality. Since 1983, the mental health professional associations have agreed that it is inappropriate to try to change a person's sexual orientation, but the controversy continues between individual practitioners.

This *Treatment Planner* has been written from the perspective that homosexuality is not a disease, but that the appropriate treatment of gay men and lesbians requires acceptance of sexual orientation and some special considerations. Our choice of chapters reflects this perspective. We have devoted chapters to certain topics for three reasons:

1. Some of the problems, such as coming out and internalized homophobia, are specific to the gay and lesbian community.
2. Other issues, such as adoption, require considerably different treatment with homosexual versus heterosexual clients.
3. Other issues, such as depression and anxiety, are common to all psychotherapy clients regardless of sexual orientation.

To work with lesbians and gay men effectively, the therapist must look at problems with a broad lens. For example, AIDS is not just a physical illness. It can lead to being stigmatized, difficulty obtaining health care, estrangement from family of origin, and child custody problems. The chapters are written to assist with untangling these kind of complicated webs and proceeding with treatment in a logical, organized fashion.

The advent of managed care and the increased demand for accountability in hospitals, clinics, and nonprofit settings has revolutionized the way mental health professionals conduct treatment. The new standard is to plan treatment from the first session specifying in observable terms what the therapist and the client are going to do to resolve the problem. Each of the chapters in this *Planner* provide behavioral definitions, long-term goals, short-term objectives, and therapeutic interventions to assist in the organizing and planning of the psychotherapeutic treatment of gay men and lesbians.

HOW TO DEVELOP A TREATMENT PLAN

The beginning of any solid treatment plan is a thorough biopsychosocial assessment. The clinician must discover not only the complaints and their severity and frequency, but examine the client's entire world of family history, medical problems, legal issues, social networks, employment, and how these interact with the presenting problems. When working with lesbians and gay men, the net needs to be cast even wider. How do clients perceive their sexual orientation? Who knows, and doesn't, about their sexuality. How is their level of openness about their identity affected by their living situation, job, and so on? It's important to evaluate the client's relationships and seek clarification of their meaning to the client. A "friend" may be a long-term life partner with whom the client shares property and child-rearing responsibilities. "Family" may be the client's network of friends. After completing the initial assessment process (the process itself continues through treatment), the clinician needs to integrate the information so that treatment can be focused and effective.

Step One: Problem Selection

This *Gay and Lesbian Psychotherapy Treatment Planner* provides treatment plans for 27 problems that are often encountered by clinicians working with this population. It is possible to have more than one problem per client. Under most circumstances, it is best to limit the problem selection to two of three problems. Anything greater than that and treatment may lose its focus. If you conceive of the treatment plan as a road map of where you are going and how you are going to get there, this logic becomes clearer. Maps of several destinations are likely to get you and your passengers lost.

Engaging the client in treatment planning is the most effective way to simplify the problem selection process, increase collaboration, and avoid future misunderstandings. The best consultant is, of course, the client. Asking clients what their perception of the problem is and what they would like to work on and toward should assist in identifying the problem.

Step Two: Problem Definition

The problem must be stated in observable, behavioral terms. Conceptualizing the problems in this way will provide direction for the rest of the treatment. By specifying the problematic behaviors, it is possible to define what should change and how. In addition, the symptom pattern should match as closely as possible the diagnostic criteria found in the *Diagnostic and Statistical Manual. The Gay and Lesbian Psychotherapy Treatment Planner* offers behaviorally specific definition statements to choose from, or to serve as a model for those you choose to write yourself.

Step Three: Goal Development

Setting goals for resolution of the defined problem is the next step in developing the treatment plan. These desired outcomes do not need to be measurable but are global, long-term goals that indicate the client has had a positive resolution to the problem presented. This *Planner* suggests several possible long-term goals for each problem, but the use of a single problem statement is all that is required in the treatment plan.

Step Four: Objective Construction

Objectives must be stated in behavioral terms that have measurable outcomes. Review agencies (e.g., JCAHO, NCQA, Insurance Companies) insist that outcomes be measurable and therefore, the objectives in this *Planner* are designed to meet this demand for accountability. Each listed problem has several options of objectives to choose from and these objectives should be used to tailor the treatment plan to the unique characteristics and needs of the client.

Objectives can be viewed as a series of steps that need to be taken in order to achieve and complete the long term goal. At least two objectives should be used for each problem but more can be used, if needed, in order to achieve the goal. Target completion dates or number of sessions needed may be attached to each objective. New objectives may be added to the treatment plan as the treatment progresses. When the client has attained all the objectives in the plan the problem should be resolved.

Step Five: Intervention Selection

The therapist must next specify which interventions are going to be employed to achieve the objectives. There should be one or more interventions for each objective. If the objective is not accomplished after the initial intervention, new interventions should be added to the treatment plan.

Interventions should be selected based on the needs of the client and the expertise of the clinician. This *Planner* contains interventions from several therapeutic approaches including pharmacological, interpersonal, psychodynamic, cognitive, behavioral, systems-oriented, social ecological, and solution-focused interventions. Other interventions may be written and used by clinicians based on their individual training and experience.

Step Six: Diagnosis Determination

The determination of an appropriate diagnosis is based on an evaluation of the client's complete clinical presentation. The clinician should gather a clear picture of the client's clinical presentation that includes cognitive, emotional, and interpersonal symptoms to compare with the *DSM-IV* criteria to determine a diagnosis of mental illness, if appropriate. The careful assessment of behaviors can facilitate a more accurate diagnosis and help in developing a more effective treatment plan.

HOW TO USE THIS PLANNER

The *Gay and Lesbian Treatment Planner* was written to be a tool for the clinician in quickly writing effective treatment plans that are customized for the gay or lesbian client. Treatment plans should be developed by moving through the following steps:

1. *Step One:* Choose one presenting problem for those identified in the assessment process. Locate the corresponding page number for that problem in *The Gay and Lesbian Psychotherapy Treatment Planner*'s contents.
2. *Step Two:* Select two or three of the listed behavioral definitions and record them in the appropriate section on your treatment plan form.
3. *Step Three:* Select one or two long-term goals, and record them in the goals section of your treatment plan form.
4. *Step Four:* Review the list of objectives for this problem and select the ones clinically indicated for the client. Remember that it is recommended that at least two objectives be selected for each problem. You may add the target date or number of sessions allocated for the attainment of each objective.
5. *Step Five:* Choose relevant interventions. The numbers of the interventions most salient to each objective are listed in parentheses following the objective statement. You may choose other interventions from the list, or add new interventions in the space provided.
6. *Step Six: DSM-IV* diagnoses that are associated with the problem are listed at the end of each chapter. These diagnoses are meant to be suggestions for clinical consideration. Select a diagnosis listed or assign a more appropriate choice from the *DSM-IV.*

Following these steps will facilitate the development of complete, customized treatment plans ready for immediate implementation and presentation to clients. The final plan should resemble the format of the sample plan presented at the end of this introduction.

ELECTRONIC TREATMENT PLANNING

As paperwork mounts, an increasing number of therapists are turning to computerized record keeping. The presenting problems, goals, objectives, interventions, and diagnoses in *The Gay and Lesbian Psychotherapy Treatment Planner* are available in electronic form as an add-on upgrade module to the popular software *TheraScribe 3.0* or *3.5 for Windows®: The Computerized Assistant to Treatment Planning.*

For more information on *TheraScribe* or *The Gay and Lesbian Treatment Planner* add-on module, call John Wiley & Sons at (800) 879-4539 or mail in the information request coupon at the back of this book.

A WORD OF CAUTION

Whether using the print *Planner* or the electronic version, *TheraScribe 3.0* or *3.5,* it is critical to remember that effective treatment planning requires that each plan be tailored to the client's problems and needs. *Treatment plans should not be mass-produced, even if clients have similar problems.* Each client's strengths and weaknesses, unique stressors, social network, family circumstances, and interactional patterns must be considered in developing a treatment strategy. The clinically-derived statements in this *Planner* can be combined in thousands of permutations to develop detailed treatment plans. In addition, readers are encouraged to add their own definitions, goals, objectives and interventions to the existing samples.

A FINAL NOTE

Our hope is that you use this book as a tool to plan and deliver effective, sensitive treatment for lesbians and gay men seeking assistance. As we mentioned earlier, the history of treatment of gay men and lesbians has been an unhappy one. By assisting you in the aim to work better, and more sensitively, we hope that this book is a step to a happier future for lesbian, gay men, and all the people whose lives they touch.

SAMPLE TREATMENT PLAN

Presenting Problem: HIV/AIDS

Behavioral Definitions

1. A positive test for human immunodeficiency virus (HIV).
2. Physical symptoms such as chronic low-grade fever, persistent fatigue, diarrhea, unintentional weight loss, skin rash, and night sweats.
3. Social withdrawal and lack of energy.

Long-Term Goals

1. Accept AIDS diagnosis/HIV status and pursue proper medical attention.

Short-Term Objectives:	Therapeutic Interventions:
1. Describe HIV/AIDS medical status openly and without denial. (7/3/99)	1. Explore the client's understanding of his/her medical status. 2. Confront the denial of the HIV/AIDS status and of the necessity for follow through with medical protocol.
2. Comply totally with doctor's orders for tests, medications, limitations, and/or treatments. (8/12/99)	1. Monitor and document client's follow through on doctor's orders and redirect when client is failing to comply. 2. Consult with physician and review doctor's orders with client.
3. Identify emotional effects of being diagnosed with HIV/AIDS. (9/3/99)	1. Help client identify and express his/her feelings connected with medical condition. 2. Assess reactions of client's social network (e.g., friends, family, coworkers) and offer conjoint or family appointments to facilitate support for client. 3. Assess and monitor suicidal behavior.

Diagnosis: 309.0 Adjustment Disorder with Depressed Mood

ADOPTION/SURROGACY

BEHAVIORAL DEFINITIONS

1. Ambivalence of a couple or individual regarding adopting or participating in artificial insemination and parenting a child.
2. Uncertainty about ability to fulfill role of parent.
3. Fear, hopelessness, confusion, and ambivalence about obtaining/rearing a child in a homophobic culture.
4. Confusion over the process and options as to how to obtain a child available to gays and lesbians.
5. Concern about the impact of child-rearing on couple's relationship.
6. Lack of agreement between partners regarding the decision to pursue adoption or surrogacy.

—. _____
   _____
—. _____
   _____
   _____
—. _____
   _____

LONG-TERM GOALS

1. Understand impact of decision to obtain a child upon individual or couple.
2. Understand available ways in which a gay or lesbian individual or couple may obtain a child.
3. Make a decision about which means to follow to obtain a child (e.g., adoption, surrogacy).
4. Take necessary steps to initiate and complete adoption or surrogacy process.

5. Develop long-term coping strategies to overcome discrimination experienced by gays and lesbians obtaining a child.
6. Understand and verbalize the emotional, legal, and financial commitments necessary to raise a child to adulthood and make decision to proceed to obtain a child.
7. Develop a plan to obtain resources (e.g., child care, social support, education, health care) to support parenting a child.
8. Provide a safe, loving environment for the adoptive child.
9. Develop and demonstrate appropriate parenting skills.

—. _____
   _____
   _____
—. _____
   _____
   _____
—. _____
   _____

SHORT-TERM OBJECTIVES

THERAPEUTIC INTERVENTIONS

1. Express emotions (e.g., fear, ambivalence, confusion) regarding decision to parent. (1, 2)

2. Verbalize an understanding of the legal issues surrounding gays and lesbians adopting children. (3, 4)

3. Write and discuss a list of advantages and disadvantages to adoption and/or surrogacy. (3, 4, 5, 6)

4. Verbalize an understanding of the ways to obtain a child. (7, 8)

5. Identify available options for adoption and list advantages and disadvantages of each option. (3, 4, 7)

1. Actively build the level of trust with the client in individual sessions through consistent eye contact, active listening, unconditional positive regard, and warm acceptance to help increase his/her ability to identify and express feelings.

2. Explore and clarify feelings associated with possible adoption/surrogacy.

3. Educate about disadvantages of different forms of adoption (e.g., public adoption has long waiting periods, private adoption is expensive, foreign adoption is expensive and difficult legally).

4. Educate about advantages of adoption (e.g., no need to

6. Verbalize an understanding of the potential legal issues regarding surrogacy. (5, 8)

7. Verbalize a decision about which form of adoption to use. (7, 9, 10, 11, 12)

8. Express mutual agreement over decision to obtain a child. (9, 10, 11, 12, 13)

9. Identify societal myths surrounding gay and lesbian people in the role of parents and verbalize an understanding of the facts. (14)

10. Verbalize an understanding of the potential discrimination that may be experienced by a child being raised by gays/lesbians. (15, 16)

11. Identify friends or family members willing and able to provide child care and/or emotional support. (17, 18)

12. Identify all elements of a support network that will assist in appropriately raising the child. (15, 17, 18, 19)

13. Express confidence in fulfilling the role of parent. (16, 17, 18, 20)

14. Develop a financial plan to adequately provide for the basic necessities of life for the child. (21, 22)

15. Identify child care options available in the community that are sensitive to gay/lesbian parents. (23, 24)

involve a third party for egg/sperm donation who may later seek custody, greater access to services).

5. Educate about disadvantages of surrogacy (e.g., involving a third party, custody issues, only one partner is the legal custodian and perceived as "real" parent).

6. Educate about advantages of surrogacy (e.g., biological connection, biological parent has custody rights, comparatively inexpensive).

7. Educate about available options for adoption (e.g., public adoption, foster-adopt programs, private agencies, independent adoption, foreign adoption) and available resources (e.g., National Adoption Information Clearing House, local public agency).

8. Educate about available options and resources for surrogacy (e.g., Surrogate Mothers Inc., Center for Reproductive Alternatives).

9. Prioritize available options by listing them in order of preference.

10. Assist in eliminating undesirable options.

11. Explore advantages and disadvantages of desirable options and encourage client to make a choice.

12. Using role reversal technique, have couple switch places and

16. Discuss parenting roles to be taken by each partner of the couple. (25, 26)

17. Verbalize the strengths and weakness the individual or each partner will have in a parenting role. (25)

18. Discuss and verbalize an understanding of information necessary for basic parenting skills. (26, 27)

19. Attend parenting classes. (27)

20. List changes necessary to provide a safe living environment for the child. (28)

21. Identify necessary steps that need to be taken to begin and complete the adoption or surrogacy process. (29)

22. Sign release of information for adoption/surrogacy agency. (30)

23. Agree to allow therapist to provide adoption/surrogacy agency with relevant personal adjustment information gathered from a psychological evaluation. (31)

24. Discuss frustrations, anger, anxiety, disappointment, hopelessness felt due to adoption waiting period. (32)

25. Verbalize emotional reaction (e.g., worry, anxiety, fear, excitement) to having child come home. (33)

26. Report the implementation of previously developed plan to parent child. (34)

discuss the issue and the thoughts and feelings associated with it from each other's perspective.

13. Have both partners agree on a time limit for the decision.

14. Educate regarding facts about homosexuals in the role of parents (e.g., homosexuals are not child molesters more often than heterosexuals, studies have shown that children raised by gays and lesbians are not any more likely to be gay or have emotional problems than children raised by heterosexuals).

15. Encourage client to contact support groups for gay and lesbian parents (e.g., Gays & Lesbians Parents Coalition International [GLPCI], Parents, Friends of Lesbians & Gays [PFLAG], Children of Lesbians And Gays Everywhere [CO-LAGE]) to learn about potential discrimination (e.g., child's conflict with denigrating peers, child's rejection by peer's parents, teachers of the child directly or indirectly treating the child unfairly).

16. Have client(s) read books regarding gay and lesbian parenting issues (e.g., *The Lesbian and Gay Parenting Handbook* by Martin and *Lesbian and Gay Families: Redefining Families in America* by Pollack).

17. Draw an Eco-Map to assist in identifying friends and/or family members willing and able to

27. Express satisfaction in the parenting role. (35)

___. _____
_____
___. _____
_____
___. _____
_____

provide child care and/or emotional support.

18. Encourage contact with friends and/or family members to discuss the role(s) each are willing to play in rearing a child.

19. Encourage active participation in organizations that support gay/lesbian parents.

20. Explore the level of confidence in meeting the challenges involved in being a gay or lesbian parent, normalizing a moderate degree of anxiety as long as it is balanced with moderate self-assurance.

21. Assist in developing a financial plan to provide for basic necessities by estimating costs of food, clothing, medical care, and so on, and determine income needed.

22. Facilitate agreement between partners regarding child care expenses and income needs.

23. Suggest interviewing child care agencies regarding attitudes about gay/lesbian parents.

24. Suggest interviewing gay/lesbian parents and people in support groups for gay and lesbian parents about their experience with child care in the community.

25. Explore the parenting role with the client(s) and what unique strengths and weaknesses of each partner that will be brought to this role (e.g., differences in discipline methods,

ability to stay home with the child).

26. Educate about basic parenting skills (e.g., stages of development, discipline, philosophy, child's need for consistency, nurture and self-esteem enhancement).

27. Have client(s) attend local parenting class(es) that are gay/lesbian sensitive, if available.

28. List and discuss changes necessary to provide safe living environment for the child (e.g., proper storage of medications, safety locks, providing child own space).

29. Encourage contact with adoption/surrogacy agency to identify steps needed to begin and complete the process.

30. Obtain a signed release of information for the adoption/surrogacy agency.

31. Conduct psychological evaluation of client(s), discuss results with client(s) and provide agency with report.

32. Explore emotional reactions (e.g., frustration, anxiety, fear) to adoption waiting period.

33. Process emotional reaction to having child come home for the first time.

34. Inquire as to success with plan that had been developed earlier to parent the child and process any changes that need to be made.

35. Probe for sources of satisfaction in the parenting role.

——. _____

_____

——. _____

_____

——. _____

_____

DIAGNOSTIC SUGGESTIONS

Axis I: 309.0   Adjustment Disorder with Depressed Mood
309.24   Adjustment Disorder with Anxiety
309.28   Adjustment Disorder with Mixed Anxiety and
Depressed Mood
313.82   Identity Problem
V61.1   Partner Relational Problem
V62.81   Partner Relational Problem NOS
V62.89   Phase of Life Problem

_____   _____

_____   _____

AGING

BEHAVIORAL DEFINITIONS

1. Recent loss of life partner.
2. Subjective experience of distress, anxiety, hopelessness over pending retirement.
3. Difficulty locating social/health services (e.g., retirement community, skilled nursing facility) which are sensitive to the needs of lesbians and gay men.
4. No outside social support (e.g., friends, family, or other sources or recreation).
5. Persistent rumination over lost youth, beauty, physical abilities, and so on.
6. Thoughts dominated by grieving loss of significant others, coupled with poor concentration, tearful spells, and confusion about the future.
7. Increase in health problems (e.g., diabetes, heart disease) which are affecting ability to maintain independence.
8. Difficulty remembering previously learned information.

___. _____
   _____
___. _____
   _____
___. _____
   _____

LONG-TERM GOALS

1. Complete grieving of life partner and engage in new relationships.
2. Eliminate any symptoms of psychological distress (e.g., anxiety, hopelessness).

3. Actively participate in a variety of services and activities which support highest level of independence.
4. Accept aging as a natural process.
5. Rebuild social support system so it is adequate to meet emotional needs.

—. _____

_____

—. _____

_____

—. _____

_____

SHORT-TERM OBJECTIVES

1. Cooperate with comprehensive biopsychosocial assessment. (1)

2. Identify any suicidal thoughts or impulses and contract not to harm self. (2, 3)

3. Cooperate with physical examination to rule out or diagnose any medical conditions and/or to determine the severity of same. (4)

4. Actively participate in psychological testing. (5)

5. Identify any substance abuse. (6)

6. Verbalize an understanding of how abusing drugs and alcohol has been a maladaptive attempt to deal with life stressors. (7)

7. Stop all drug and alcohol abuse. (8)

8. Utilize external memory aids and coping strategies. (9)

THERAPEUTIC INTERVENTIONS

1. Conduct comprehensive bio-psychosocial assessment focusing upon client's current level of functioning, history of complaint, and client's perception of problem.

2. Conduct a suicide assessment and encourage client to endorse no-harm contract. (See Depression chapter in this *Planner*.)

3. Assess and monitor suicide potential, referring client to a more restrictive level of care if necessary for personal safety.

4. Refer client to medical doctor to rule out any medical conditions and/or determine the severity of same.

5. Conduct neuropsychological testing to assist with identifying any neurological conditions which are contributing to deterioration of cognitive functioning.

9. Verbalize the disturbing negative emotions related to aging. (10, 11)

10. Keep a daily record of dysfunctional thinking that includes each situation associated with depressed feelings and the thoughts that triggered those feelings. (11, 12)

11. Implement positive, realistic thoughts that counteract negative emotions. (13)

12. List 10 positive aspects of aging. (14)

13. Identify the impact of the death of significant others upon social support. (15)

14. Share emotions and experiences related to loss of significant others. (15, 16, 17, 18)

15. Participate in life review to resolve grief issues. (18)

16. Watch movies related to aging among gay men and lesbians. (19)

17. Identify resources (e.g., meals on wheels, nursing assistants) which can assist in maintaining independence. (20)

18. Participate in social activities designed for aging lesbians and/or gay men. (21, 22, 23)

19. Increase level of social interaction. (22, 23)

20. Identify sources of spiritual support. (24)

21. Participate in religious/spiritual activities which increase sense of well-being. (25)

6. Conduct a substance abuse assessment including substances taken, amount, frequency, and any consequences (e.g., arrests, relationship problems) that have occurred as a result.

7. Assist client in recognizing how using substances has been an attempt to deal with life stressors; identify the negative consequences of the substance abuse.

8. Refer client to or provide drug and alcohol treatment services (e.g., outpatient, day treatment, intensive outpatient, AA/NA). (See Chemical Dependence chapter of this *Planner*.)

9. Assign and monitor enhancing activities/exercises (e.g., working a crossword puzzle, playing memory games) and memory loss coping strategies.

10. Explore the client's negative emotions (e.g., hopelessness, anxiety, sadness) related to aging.

11. Assist client in developing awareness of cognitive messages that reinforce hopelessness and helplessness.

12. Direct the client to keep a daily record that lists each situation associated with the depressed feelings and the dysfunctional thinking that triggered the depression.

13. Use logic and reality to challenge dysfunctional thoughts for accuracy, replacing them

___. _____
   _____
___. _____
   _____
___. _____
   _____

with positive, accurate thoughts.

14. Assign client in listing 10 positive aspects of aging (e.g., not having to work, relation- ships stronger, not having to deal with coming out issues). Process in session with therapist.

15. Assist client with drawing an Eco-Map or genogram detail- ing social support network before and after death of significant others and process with therapist.

16. Assign client to keep a daily grief journal to be shared in therapy sessions.

17. Ask client to bring pictures or mementos connected with de- ceased significant others to a session and talk about them with therapist. (See Grief/ Multiple Loss chapter in this *Planner*.)

18. Conduct life review with client in which he/she remembers key events (e.g., holidays, relation- ships, traumas) to assist in grieving losses and focusing upon memories which are still intact.

19. Assign client homework of watching movies depicting aging lesbians and/or gay men (e.g., An Empty Bed, Nitrate Kisses); process thoughts and feelings precipitated by the experience.

20. Educate client regarding services available to assist him/her in maintaining independence.

21. Refer client to social service organizations that provide activities for senior lesbians and/or gay men (e.g., Senior Active in a Gay Environment, Gay and Lesbian Association of Retired People).

22. Reinforce social activities and verbalization of feelings, needs, and desires.

23. Assist client in developing a social activity plan and encourage its implementation.

24. Assist client in identifying spiritual sources of support (e.g., temple, church, 12-Step group, meditation group) which would fulfill spiritual needs.

25. Positively reinforce client's participation in spiritual/religious groups which increase sense of well-being. (See Religious Conflicts chapter in this *Planner*.)

__. _____
   _____
__. _____
   _____
__. _____
   _____

DIAGNOSTIC SUGGESTIONS

Axis I:

309.0	Adjustment Disorder with Depressed Mood
309.28	Adjustment Disorder with Mixed Anxiety and Depressed Mood
300.00	Anxiety Disorder NOS
309.24	Adjustment Disorder with Anxiety
V62.82	Bereavement
290.10	Dementia due to Creutzfeldt-Jakob Disease
294.9	Dementia due to HIV Disease
294.1	Dementia due to Parkinson's Disease
294.1	Dementia Due to [Indicate Other General Medical Condition]
296.2	Major Depressive Disorder, Single Episode
296.3	Major Depressive Disorder, Recurrent
300.4	Dysthymic Disorder
313.82	Identity Problem
_____	_____
_____	_____

Axis II:

301.81	Narcissistic Personality Disorder
301.50	Histrionic Personality Disorder
_____	_____
_____	_____

ANXIETY*

BEHAVIORAL DEFINITIONS

1. Excessive and persistent, daily worry about several life circumstances that have no factual or logical basis.
2. Symptoms of motor tension such as restlessness, tiredness, shakiness, or muscle tension.
3. Symptoms of autonomic hyperactivity such as palpitations, shortness of breath, dry mouth, trouble swallowing, nausea, or diarrhea.
4. Symptoms of hypervigilance such as feeling constantly on edge, concentration difficulties, trouble falling or staying asleep, and general state of irritability.

—. _____
   _____
—. _____
   _____
—. _____
   _____

LONG-TERM GOALS

1. Reduce overall level, frequency, and intensity of the anxiety so that daily functioning is not impaired.
2. Stabilize anxiety level while increasing ability to function on a daily basis.
3. Resolve the core conflict that is the source of anxiety.
4. Enhance ability to handle effectively the full variety of life's anxieties.

*From Jongsma, A.E., and Peterson, L.M., *The Complete Adult Psychotherapy Treatment Planner* (New York: John Wiley & Sons, Inc., 1999). © 1999 by Arthur E. Jongsma, Jr., and L. Mark Peterson. Reprinted with permission.

—. _____
   _____
   _____
—. _____
   _____
   _____
—. _____
   _____
   _____

SHORT-TERM OBJECTIVES

1. Tell the story of the anxiety complete with ways he/she has attempted to resolve it and the suggestions others have given. (1, 2)

2. Identify major life conflicts from the past and present. (3, 4)

3. Complete anxiety homework exercises that identify cognitive distractions that generate anxious feelings. (5)

4. Complete physical evaluation for medications. (6)

5. Take medications as prescribed and report any side effects to appropriate professionals. (7)

6. Develop appropriate relaxation and diversion activities to decrease level of anxiety. (8, 9, 10)

7. Increase daily social and vocational involvement. (11)

8. Identify how worries are irrational. (12, 13)

9. Increase understanding of beliefs and messages that produce worry and anxiety. (13, 14)

THERAPEUTIC INTERVENTIONS

1. Build a level of trust with patient and create a supportive environment which will facilitate a description of his/her fears.

2. Probe with questions (see *Anxiety Disorders and Phobias* by Beck, Emery, and Greenberg) which require the patient to produce evidence of the anxiety and logical reasons for its being present.

3. Ask patient to develop and process a list of key past and present life conflicts.

4. Assist patient in becoming aware of key unresolved life conflicts and in starting to work toward their resolution.

5. Assign patient to complete and process with therapist, the anxiety section exercises in *Ten Days to Self-Esteem* (Burns).

6. Make a referral to a physician for a medication consultation.

7. Monitor medication compliance, side effects, and effectiveness. Confer with physician regularly.

10. Verbalize insight into how past traumatic experiences are causing anxiety in present un-related circumstances. (15)

11. Decrease daily level of anxiety by developing positive self-talk. (16)

12. Implement thought-stopping technique to interrupt anxiety-producing thoughts. (17)

13. List the advantages and disad-vantages of the anxiety. (18)

14. Verbalize positive principles that reduce anxious thoughts. (19)

15. Verbalize alternative positive views of reality that are incom-patible with anxiety-producing views. (20)

16. Identify an anxiety-coping mechanism that has been suc-cessful in the past and increase its use. (21)

17. Utilize paradoxical interven-tion to reduce anxiety response. (22)

—. _____
   _____
—. _____
   _____
—. _____
   _____

8. Train in guided imagery for anxiety relief.

9. Utilize biofeedback techniques to facilitate relaxation skills.

10. Assign or allow patient to choose a chapter in *Relaxation and Stress Reduction Workbook* (Davis, Robbins-Eshelman, McKay, & Eshel-man) then work with him/her to implement the chosen technique.

11. Assist patient in developing coping strategies (e.g., in-creased social involvement, obtaining employment, physi-cal exercise) for his/her anxiety.

12. Assist patient in developing an awareness of the irrational na-ture of his/her fears.

13. Analyze the fear with the pa-tient by examining the prob-ability of the negative expectation occurring, so what if it happens, ability to control it, the worst possible outcome and patient's ability to accept it. (See *Anxiety Disorders and Phobias* by Beck & Emery.)

14. Explore cognitive messages that mediate anxiety response and retrain in adaptive cognitions.

15. Reinforce insights into past emotional issues and present anxiety.

16. Help patient develop reality-based, positive cognitive mes-sages that will increase self-

confidence in coping with irrational fears.

17. Teach patient to implement a thought-stopping technique that cognitively interferes with obsessions by thinking of a stop sign and then a pleasant scene. Monitor and encourage patient's use of technique in daily life between sessions.

18. Ask patient to complete and process with therapist "Cost-Benefit Analysis" exercise (see *Ten Days to Self-Esteem* by Burns) in which he/she lists the advantages and disadvantages of the negative thought, fear, or anxiety.

19. Read and process a fable from *Friedman's Fables* (Friedman) that pertains to anxiety with the patient.

20. Reframe the fear or anxiety by offering another way of looking at it, various alternatives or by enlarging the perspective.

21. Utilize a brief solution-focused therapy approach in which the patient is probed to find a time or situation in his/her life when he/she handled the specific anxiety or an anxiety in general. Clearly focus the approach he/she used and then encourage the patient to increase the use of this. Monitor and modify the solution as required.

22. Develop a paradoxical intervention (see *Ordeal Therapy* by Haley) in which the patient

is encouraged to have the problem (e.g., anxiety) and then schedule that anxiety to occur at specific intervals each day in a specific way and for a defined length of time. It is best to have it happen at a time of day/night when the patient would be clearly wanting to do something else.

___. _____
_____
___. _____
_____
___. _____
_____

DIAGNOSTIC SUGGESTIONS

Axis I:	300.02	Generalized Anxiety Disorder
	300.00	Anxiety Disorder NOS
	309.24	Adjustment Disorder with Anxiety
	_____	_____
	_____	_____

BREAST CANCER

BEHAVIORAL DEFINITIONS

1. A medical diagnosis of breast cancer.
2. Physical symptoms such as pain, lethargy, or nausea related to breast cancer and/or its treatment.
3. Feelings of hopelessness, fear, anxiety, and anger.
4. Lack of interest in, or enjoyment of, social activities which were previously a source of enjoyment and satisfaction.
5. Not taking medications as prescribed nor following through with recommended chemotherapy.
6. Preoccupation with physical appearance because of mastectomy.
7. Avoidance of physical intimacy partner because of negative body image related to mastectomy.

___. _____
    _____
___. _____
    _____
___. _____
    _____

LONG-TERM GOALS

1. Medically stabilize physical condition.
2. Increased knowledge of breast cancer and medical treatment options.
3. Return to level of emotional, occupational, and social functioning present before diagnosis.
4. Participation in a wide range of social activities that are supportive and rewarding.

5. Improve communication with partner, friends, family, and other sources of social support about the disease process and related emotions.
6. Accept self and body, demonstrating no hesitancy to participate in physical intimacy with partner.

—. _____
_____
_____

—. _____
_____
_____

—. _____
_____

SHORT-TERM OBJECTIVES

1. Describe medical status openly and without minimization or denial. (1)

2. Identify any homophobic and/or sexist attitudes or behaviors of health care providers that have caused feelings of hopelessness, despair, anger, and so on. (2)

3. Identify any barriers that are limiting access to health care. (2, 3)

4. Verbalize an understanding of the resources available to overcome barriers to accessing health care. (4)

5. Decrease level of verbal denial regarding health status and/or cancer diagnosis while increasing level of verbal acceptance. (5)

6. List questions about breast cancer that have not been answered. (6)

THERAPEUTIC INTERVENTIONS

1. Actively build working relationship by demonstrating unconditional positive regard, making empathetic statements, and remaining nonjudgmental while exploring client's experience with breast cancer.

2. Explore about experiences with homophobia and sexism. Encourage expression of emotions related to these experiences.

3. Assist client in identifying all barriers (e.g., no health insurance, lack of transportation, homophobic physicians) to health care.

4. Educate client about the resources available to overcome barriers to health care (e.g., public health programs for low-income people, medical referrals through Gay and Lesbian Medical Associations, bus fares for disabled).

7. Ask health care providers questions about cancer and its treatment. (7, 8, 9)

8. Report an increased knowledge of breast cancer and its treatment as a result of consulting books, magazines, and Internet sites. (10, 11, 12)

9. Identify any legal problems and take all steps necessary to eliminate them. (13, 14)

10. Write a plan for medical treatment and self-care. (15)

11. Comply completely with plan for medical care and self-care. (16, 17)

12. Verbalize the feelings associated with breast cancer diagnosis. (18)

13. Cooperate with assessment for suicidality and depression. (19)

14. Verbalize worries, thoughts, and concerns related to mastectomy. (20)

15. Identify negative automatic thoughts that contribute to feelings of helplessness and hopelessness and replace with more realistic, positive messages. (21, 22, 23)

16. Verbalize hopeful statements about the future. (21, 22, 23)

17. Identify how emotions and behaviors have negatively affected health. (24)

18. Partner will actively participate in conjoint sessions to provide support and increase communication. (25)

5. Confront regarding denial of health status and avoidance of pursuing health care while reinforcing realistic acceptance of breast cancer diagnosis and treatment options.

6. Assist client in developing a list of questions that have not been answered about diagnosis, treatment, side-effects, and so on.

7. Using role play, modeling, and behavioral rehearsal, teach assertiveness skills that can be applied to being an active participant in decisions regarding breast cancer treatment.

8. Role play asking questions of physician (e.g., "What are my chances for survival?" "How long do I need to be in chemotherapy?" and "What are my treatment options?") in session. Provide positive reinforcement as client demonstrates increased ability to ask difficult questions.

9. Assign client to become better informed regarding breast cancer, the treatment options, and prognosis, and so on by assertively asking questions of health care providers.

10. Recommend reading books that provide information about breast cancer (e.g., *The Lesbian Health Book* by White & Martinez and *Dr. Susan Love's Breast Book*).

11. Encourage subscribing to and reading magazines that provide

19. Verbalize feelings to partner directly in session. (26)

20. Verbalize an understanding of how cancer has affected couple's functioning. (27, 28)

21. Resolve any partner conflicts that are contributing to distress and/or difficulty following self-care plan. (28)

22. Identify people who can be sources of emotional support. (29, 30)

23. Utilize Internet chat rooms and bulletin boards that are focused on breast cancer to broaden support network. (31)

24. Attend breast cancer support group. (32)

25. Utilize relaxation or meditation techniques to reduce stress. (33)

26. Report instances of using laughter to reduce anxiety and tension. (34, 35)

27. Identify life priorities, goals, and aspirations, and develop a specific plan for implementing these. (36)

28. Participate in breast cancer political activities to increase sense of empowerment. (37)

___. _____
   _____

___. _____
   _____

___. _____
   _____

information about cancer and its treatment (e.g., *MAMM: Women, Cancer and Community*).

12. Refer to reputable Internet sites (e.g., Cancernet.nci.nih.gov or www.cancernews.com/breast.htm) that provide information about breast cancer.

13. Assist client in identifying current of potential legal problems (e.g., custody arrangements, wills, durable powers of attorney) and encourage taking all necessary steps to resolve them.

14. Refer to attorney for assistance with resolving legal problems. (See Legal Conflicts chapter in this *Planner*.)

15. Assign the writing of a plan for care that includes treatment options that will be pursued, who will provide medical care, and who will assist client in providing emotional support and assistance with activities of daily living.

16. Monitor and document adherence with self-care plan and redirect when client is failing to comply.

17. Consult with physician and review doctor's orders with client.

18. Explore feelings related to breast cancer diagnosis.

19. Assess for signs and symptoms of depression and suicidality, referring to psychiatrist for

medications if indicated. (See Depression chapter in this *Planner.*)

20. Assist client in expressing worries, thoughts, (e.g., No one will love me, I'll be permanently disfigured, I would rather not have the operation) and concerns regarding mastectomy.

21. Educate about the use of an automatic thought record and assist in identifying negative thoughts.

22. Assist client in developing positive messages to replace distortions that lead to helplessness and hopelessness.

23. Assign client to complete and process exercises on thought distortion related to helplessness and depression in *Ten Days to Self-Esteem* (Burns).

24. Assign listing the negative emotions and behaviors that have had a deleterious consequence to health; process changes (e.g., improved nutrition, exercise, stop smoking, regular sleep pattern, positive attitude and outlook) that would benefit health.

25. Encourage client to include his/her partner in conjoint sessions to strengthen bond of support and promote understanding and communication.

26. Encourage expressing fears, concerns, and anxieties to partner in session. Process partner's reactions.

27. Have both partners read *Cancer in Two Voices* (Butler & Rosenblaum) to increase their understanding of the impact of breast cancer upon the couple's functioning. Process reactions in session.

28. Facilitate resolution to conflicts between partners. (See Intimate Partner Conflicts chapter of this *Planner.*)

29. Have client draw an Eco-Map to assist in identifying people who are potential sources of support and encourage client to enlist their help.

30. Assess reactions of client's social network (e.g., friends, family, coworkers) to cancer diagnosis/treatment and offer conjoint or family sessions to facilitate support for client.

31. Educate about on-line sources of support (e.g., Internet chat rooms, bulletin boards) and encourage their use.

32. Refer to breast cancer support group for lesbians (or one that is sensitive to their needs).

33. Train in relaxation and/or meditation techniques to reduce stress.

34. Recommend reading *You Can Fight for Your Life* (LeShan) and/or *Anatomy of an Illness* (Cousins) to increase understanding of the therapeutic impact of laughter and reinforce progress toward developing a positive attitude.

35. Encourage client to watch comedic movies, videos, and so on, that assist in alleviating stress. Inquire as to impact on mood in session.

36. Assign client to list "unfinished tasks" and develop a plan for completing them.

37. Educate about political and social activities that will assist in increasing a sense of empowerment (e.g., Breast Cancer Awareness Month, Lesbian Health Projects, Feminist Health Centers).

__. _____

_____

__. _____

_____

__. _____

_____

DIAGNOSTIC SUGGESTIONS

Axis I:	309.24	Adjustment Disorder with Anxiety
	309.0	Adjustment Disorder with Depressed Mood
	309.28	Adjustment Disorder with Mixed Anxiety and Depressed Mood
	296.2x	Major Depressive Disorder, Single Episode
	296.3x	Major Depressive Disorder, Recurrent
	300.02	Generalized Anxiety Disorder
	316	[Specified Psychological Factor] Affecting . . . [Indicate the General Medical Condition]
	316	Maladaptive Health Behaviors Affecting . . . [Indicate the General Medical Condition]
	300.4	Dysthymic Disorder
	V15.81	Noncompliance with Treatment
	_____	_____
	_____	_____

CHEMICAL DEPENDENCE

BEHAVIORAL DEFINITIONS

1. Maladaptive pattern of substance use manifested by increased tolerance and withdrawal.
2. Inability to stop or reduce use of mood-altering drug despite the verbalized desire to do so and the negative consequences of continued use.
3. Blood work (e.g., elevated liver enzymes, electrolyte imbalance) and physical indicators (e.g., stomach pain, high blood pressure, malnutrition) reflect a pattern of heavy substance abuse.
4. Denial that chemical dependence is a problem despite feedback from significant others that the substance use is negatively affecting him or her.
5. Frequent blackouts when using.
6. Continued substance use despite persistent physical, legal, financial, vocational, social, or relationship problems that are directly caused by the substance use.
7. Drug/alcohol tolerance increases as increased substance use is required to become intoxicated or to obtain the desired drug effect.
8. Physical withdrawal symptoms (e.g., shaking, seizures, nausea, headaches, sweating, anxiety, insomnia, and/or depression) when going without the substance for any length of time.
9. Arrests for substance abuse-related offenses (e.g., driving under the influence, minor in possession, assault, possession/delivery of a controlled substance, shoplifting).
10. Suspension of important social, recreational, or occupational activities because they interfere with drug/alcohol use.
11. Large time investment in activities to obtain the substance, use it, or recover from its effects.
12. Consumption of substance in greater amounts for longer periods of time than intended.

—. _____
_____
—. _____
_____
—. _____
_____

LONG-TERM GOALS

1. Accept chemical dependence and begin to actively participate in a recovery program.
2. Establish a sustained recovery, free from the use of all mood-altering substances.
3. Establish and maintain total abstinence while increasing knowledge of addiction and the process of recovery.
4. Acquire the skills necessary to maintain long-term sobriety from all mood-altering substances and live a life free of chemicals.
5. Improve quality of life by maintaining abstinence from all mood-altering chemicals.
6. Withdraw from mood-altering substance, stabilize physically and emotionally, and then establish a supportive recovery plan.

—. _____
_____
—. _____
_____
—. _____
_____

SHORT-TERM OBJECTIVES

1. Provide honest and complete information for chemical dependence biopsychosocial history. (1, 2)

2. Cooperate with a medical examination. (2)

THERAPEUTIC INTERVENTIONS

1. Gather a complete drug/alcohol history including amount and pattern of use, signs and symptoms of use, and negative life consequences (e.g., social, legal, familial, vocational) resulting from client's chemical dependence.

3. List 10 negative consequences resulting from or exacerbated by substance dependence. (3, 4, 5)

4. Verbalize how drugs and alcohol increase the risk of contracting HIV and other sexually transmitted diseases. (4)

5. Identify the ways being sober could positively impact life. (5)

6. Read assigned material to increase knowledge of addiction and the process of recovery. (6)

7. Verbalize an increased knowledge of the addiction and recovery process. (6, 7, 8, 9, 10)

8. Identify sources of on-going support in maintaining sobriety that are supportive of gay men and lesbians. (6, 7, 8, 9, 10)

9. Attend a self-help group to support sobriety. (7, 8, 9, 10)

10. Write a substance abuse-recovery plan. (11)

11. Verbalize a recognition of how mood-altering chemicals were used as a coping mechanism to escape from stress or pain, and their use resulted in negative consequences. (12)

12. List the negative emotions that were caused or exacerbated by substance dependence. (13)

13. Identify steps to be taken to eliminate negative emotions caused by substance abuse. (14)

14. List the social, emotional, and family factors that contributed

2. Refer client for thorough physical examination to determine if there are any physical consequences of chemical dependence and whether or not medical assistance is needed for detoxification.

3. Ask the client to list 10 ways chemical use has negatively impacted life and process with the therapist.

4. Educate the client about his/her higher risk of contracting HIV and other sexually transmitted diseases (e.g., less likely to use condoms, more sexual partners, sharing intravenous needles) when using drugs and alcohol and confront any minimizing of risk.

5. Ask the client how his/her life would be different if he/she were abstinent from alcohol/drugs.

6. Ask the patient to read Chapter 8 of *Growing Up Gay in a Dysfunctional Family* (Isensee) or the book *Easing the Ache* (Crawford).

7. Assess client's reaction to spiritual aspects of 12-Step groups and educate the client about the availability of AA/NA meetings for gay men and lesbians in the community.

8. Educate client about alternatives to 12-Step groups (Rational Recovery and Secular Organizations for Sobriety).

9. Recommend client attend community support groups to

to substance dependence. (15, 16)

15. List all lies used to hide substance dependence. (17)

16. Practice healthy communication skills to reduce stress and increase positive social interaction. (18)

17. Practice problem-solving skills. (19)

18. Verbalize options to substance abuse in dealing with stress. (20)

19. Identify constructive pleasurable activities that will replace the vacuum created by termination of substance-related activities. (21, 22, 23)

20. Practice stress management skills to reduce overall stress levels, relax, and feel comfortable. (24)

21. Identify potential relapse triggers. (25, 26)

22. Practice and implement the use of assertiveness to cope with pressure to use mood-altering substances. (27)

23. List 10 distraction behaviors to use to cope with craving for drug/alcohol use. (28)

24. Identify strategies for constructively dealing with each potential relapse trigger. (27, 28, 29)

25. Meet with significant others and have them verbalize an understanding of their role in the

maintain sobriety (e.g., Alcoholics Anonymous, Narcotics Anonymous, Rational Recovery, and Secular Organizations for Sobriety) and report to therapist the impact of meetings.

10. Assign client to meet with a gay/lesbian member of their community support group who has been abstinent from drugs and alcohol for several years and find out specifically how the program has helped him/her stay sober.

11. Assign and review client's substance abuse recovery plan to ensure it is adequate to maintain sobriety.

12. Explore substance abuse as an escape from stress, physical, and emotional pain and boredom; confronting the negative consequences of this pattern of behavior.

13. Probe the sense of shame, guilt, and low self-worth that has resulted from substance abuse.

14. Assist client in identifying the steps necessary to eliminate negative emotions that have resulted from substance abuse (e.g., consistent sobriety, making amends with others, forgiving self, reordering priorities, feeling forgiven from higher power).

15. Probe the client's family history for chemical dependence patterns and relate these to the client's use.

disease and the recovery process. (30, 31, 32, 33)

26. List 10 ways chemical dependence has caused pain to significant others and share this with them in a joint appointment. (34)

27. Significant others verbally identify their enabling behaviors. (33, 35)

28. Significant others state a plan of how to support client's recovery. (36)

__. _____
   _____
__. _____
   _____
__. _____
   _____

16. Explore the client's pattern of use in gay/lesbian bars and assist him/her in identifying how this environment contributed to using drugs/alcohol.

17. Have the client list all lies he/she told to hide substance abuse. Explore with client how this "enabled" the addiction to continue.

18. Use role-playing, modeling, and behavioral rehearsal to teach the client healthy communication skills (e.g., using "I" messages, reflecting, active listening, empathy, sharing).

19. Use modeling, role-playing, and behavioral rehearsal to teach the client how to solve problems in an organized fashion (e.g., write the problem, think accurately, list the options of action, evaluate the pros and cons of each alternative, act, monitor results).

20. Help the client to clarify how he/she was using substances and identify other constructive ways to achieve stress reduction (e.g., relaxation, positive self-talk, exercise, sharing with a friend or AA group, problem solving) to cope with stress.

21. Ask client to complete the *Inventory of Rewarding Activities* (Birchler & Weiss, 1977) to generate a list of desired activities.

22. Have the client list the pleasurable activities he/she plans to use in recovery.

23. Educate the client about sober alternatives to gay/lesbian bars for socialization and encourage him/her to explore these.

24. Using progressive relaxation techniques, teach the client how to relax and suggest that he/she practice this technique daily.

25. Assign client to do a focused autobiography from first attempts to get sober to present. Then read it for feedback as to triggers for relapse.

26. Teach the client about high-risk situations (e.g., negative emotions, social pressure, social anxiety, celebrations, interpersonal conflict, positive emotions, and testing personal control) and ask him/her to identify instances from his/her own experience when these situations triggered substance abuse.

27. Using modeling, role-playing, and behavioral rehearsal, teach the client how to assertively say no to alcohol and drugs, then practice saying no in high risk situations.

28. Have the client list 10 distraction techniques to use when experiencing craving for drugs/alcohol (e.g., going for a walk, calling a friend/sponsor, taking a bath).

29. Help the client write a plan to cope (e.g., attend a support group meeting, call a sponsor, practice relaxation, utilize

spiritual resources, exercise) with each high-risk situation that he/she has identified.

30. Ask the client's significant others to attend a session.

31. Request the client's significant others attend Al-Anon, Nar-Anon meetings.

32. Teach the client's significant others about the dynamics of enabling and tough love.

33. Monitor the client's significant others for enabling behaviors and redirect them in the session as appropriate.

34. Have the client list 10 ways in which he/she has hurt the people he/she loves because of chemical dependency and then take responsibility for it by sharing with these people in session.

35. Assign appropriate reading that will increase the significant other's knowledge of the disease, the concept of enabling, and recovery process.

36. Help the significant other develop individual relapse-prevention plans for the client and facilitate a session where plans are shared with the chemically dependent client.

__. _____

_____

__. _____

_____

__. _____

_____

DIAGNOSTIC SUGGESTIONS

Axis I:	305.00	Alcohol Abuse
	303.90	Alcohol Dependence
	305.70	Amphetamine Abuse
	304.40	Amphetamine Dependence
	305.20	Cannabis Abuse
	304.30	Cannabis Dependence
	305.60	Cocaine Abuse
	304.20	Cocaine Dependence
	305.50	Opioid Abuse
	304.00	Opioid Dependence
	304.80	Polysubstance Dependence
	304.10	Sedative, Hypnotic, or Anxiolytic Dependence
	_____	_____
	_____	_____
Axis II:	301.7	Antisocial Personality Disorder
	301.83	Borderline Personality Disorder
	301.81	Narcissistic Personality Disorder
	_____	_____
	_____	_____

DEPRESSION*

BEHAVIORAL DEFINITIONS

1. Loss of appetite.
2. Depressed affect.
3. Diminished interest in or enjoyment of activities.
4. Psychomotor agitation or retardation.
5. Sleeplessness or hypersomnia.
6. Lack of energy.
7. Poor concentration and indecisiveness.
8. Social withdrawal.
9. Suicidal thoughts and/or gestures.
10. Feelings of hopelessness, worthlessness, or inappropriate guilt.
11. Low self-esteem.
12. Unresolved grief issues.
13. Mood-related hallucinations or delusions.
14. History of chronic or recurrent depression which was treated with antidepressant medication, hospitalization, outpatient treatment, or a course of electroconvulsive therapy.

—. _____

_____

—. _____

_____

—. _____

_____

*From Jongsma, A.E., and Peterson, L.M., *The Complete Adult Psychotherapy Treatment Planner* (New York: John Wiley & Sons, Inc., 1999). © 1999 by Arthur E. Jongsma, Jr., and L. Mark Peterson. Reprinted with permission.

LONG-TERM GOALS

1. Alleviate depressed mood and return to previous level of effective functioning.
2. Develop the ability to recognize, accept, and cope with feelings of depression.
3. Develop healthy cognitive patterns and beliefs about self and the world that lead to alleviation of depression symptoms.
4. Appropriately grieve the loss of partner in order to normalize mood and to return to previous adaptive level of functioning.

—. _____
_____
_____

—. _____
_____
_____

—. _____
_____

SHORT-TERM OBJECTIVES

1. Describe the signs and symptoms of depression that are experienced. (1, 3)

2. Verbally identify, if possible, the source of depressed mood. (2, 3)

3. Begin to experience sadness in session while discussing the disappointment related to the loss or pain from the past. (3, 4)

4. Express feelings of hurt, disappointment, shame, and anger that are associated with early life experiences. (3, 4, 5, 6, 7)

5. Verbally express understanding of the relationship between depressed mood and repression of feelings—that is, anger, hurt, sadness, and so on. (5, 6, 7)

THERAPEUTIC INTERVENTIONS

1. Explore how depression is experienced in client's day-to-day living.

2. Ask client to make a list of what he/she is depressed about and process list with therapist.

3. Encourage client to share feelings of depression in order to clarify them and gain insight as to causes.

4. Explore experiences from the client's childhood that contribute to current depressed state.

5. Encourage client to share feelings of anger regarding pain inflicted on him/her in childhood that contributes to current depressed state.

6. Take prescribed medications responsibly at times ordered by physician. (8, 9)

7. Report to appropriate professional the effectiveness of medications and any side effects. (9)

8. Complete psychological testing to assess the depth of depression and the need for antidepressant medication and suicide prevention measures. (10)

9. Verbalize any history of suicide attempts and any current suicidal urges. (10, 11)

10. Identify cognitive self-talk that is engaged in to support depression. (12)

11. Keep a daily record of dysfunctional thinking that includes each situation associated with depressed feelings and the thoughts that triggered those feelings. (12, 13)

12. Replace negative and self-defeating self-talk with verbalization of realistic and positive cognitive messages. (13, 14, 30)

13. State no longer having thoughts of self-harm. (15, 16)

14. Show evidence of daily care for personal grooming and hygiene with minimal reminders from others. (17)

15. Make positive statements regarding self and ability to cope with stresses of life. (14, 18)

6. Explain a connection between client's previously unexpressed (repressed) feelings of anger (and helplessness) and current state of depression.

7. Suggest client read *Growing up Gay in a Dysfunctional Family* (Isensee).

8. Refer to physician to give a physical examination to rule out organic causes for depression, assess need for antidepressant medication and arrange for a prescription, if appropriate.

9. Monitor and evaluate client's medication compliance and the effectiveness of the medications on level of functioning.

10. Arrange for administration of Beck Depression Inventory, Minnesota Multiphasic Personality Inventory-2, Modified Scale for Suicidal Ideation or other objective assessment instrument. Evaluate results and give feedback to client.

11. Explore client's history and current state of suicidal urges and behavior.

12. Assist in developing client's awareness of cognitive messages that reinforce hopelessness and helplessness.

13. Help the client keep a daily record that lists each situation associated with the depressed feelings and the dysfunctional thinking that triggered the depression. Then use logic and reality to challenge each

16. Verbalize hopeful and positive statements regarding the future. (14, 18, 19)

17. Utilize behavioral strategies to overcome depression. (20, 21, 22)

18. Engage in physical and recreational activities that reflect increased energy and interest. (20, 22)

19. Participate in social contacts and initiate communication of needs and desires. (20, 23)

20. Verbalize any unresolved grief issues that may be contributing to depression. (24)

21. Read books on overcoming depression. (25)

22. Use positive conflict resolution skills to resolve interpersonal discord and to make needs and expectations known. (26, 27)

23. Increase frequency of assertive behaviors to express needs, desires, and expectations. (23, 28)

24. Decrease frequency of negative self-descriptive statements and increase frequency of positive self-descriptive statements. (18, 29, 30, 32)

25. Keep a daily journal of experiences, thoughts, and feelings to clarify instances of distorted negative thinking or perception that precipitate depressive emotions. (31, 32)

dysfunctional thought for accuracy, replacing it with a positive, accurate thought.

14. Reinforce positive, reality-based cognitive messages that enhance self-confidence and increase adaptive action.

15. Assess and monitor client's suicide potential.

16. Arrange for hospitalization, as necessary, when client is judged to be harmful to self.

17. Monitor and redirect client on daily grooming and hygiene.

18. Assign client to write at least one positive affirmation statement daily regarding himself or herself and the future.

19. Assist in teaching client more about depression and accepting some sadness as a normal variation in feeling.

20. Assist client in developing coping strategies (e.g., more physical exercise, less internal focus, increased social involvement, more assertiveness, greater need sharing, more anger expression) for feelings of depression.

21. Assign chemically dependent client to read passages related to depression from the books *One Day at a Time* (Hallinan) and *Each Day a New Beginning* (Hazelden Staff).

22. Develop a plan for client's participation in recreational activities.

___. _____
      _____
___. _____
      _____
___. _____
      _____

23. Reinforce client's social activities and verbalization of feelings, needs, and desires.

24. Explore the role of unresolved grief issues as they contribute to client's current depression. (See Interventions suggested for Grief/Loss Unresolved in this *Planner* if applicable).

25. Recommend self-help books on coping with depression [e.g., *The Feeling Good Handbook* by Burns, *What to Say When You Talk to Yourself* (Helmstetter) or *Talking to Yourself* (Butler)].

26. Teach the client conflict resolution skills (e.g., empathy, active listening, "I" messages, respectful communication, assertiveness without aggression, compromise); then use modeling, role playing, and behavior rehearsal to work through several current conflicts.

27. In conjoint sessions, help the client resolve interpersonal conflicts and problems. (See Intimate Partner Conflict chapter in this *Planner.*)

28. Use modeling and/or role playing to train client in assertiveness. If indicated refer to an assertiveness training class/group for further instruction.

29. Assign exercise of client talking positively about self into a mirror once per day.

30. Reinforce client's positive statements made about self.

31. Assign client to keep a daily journal of experiences, automatic negative thoughts associated with experiences, and the depressive affect that results from that distorted interpretation. Process journal material to diffuse destructive thinking patterns and replace with alternate, realistic, positive thoughts.

32. Explore the role that internalized homophobia plays in contributing to the client's current depression. (See Internalized Homophobia chapter in this *Planner*.)

—. _____
   _____
—. _____
   _____
—. _____
   _____

DIAGNOSTIC SUGGESTIONS

Axis I:	309.0	Adjustment Disorder with Depressed Mood
	296.xx	Bipolar I Disorder
	296.89	Bipolar II Disorder
	300.4	Dysthymic Disorder
	301.13	Cyclothymic Disorder
	296.2x	Major Depressive Disorder Single Episode
	296.3x	Major Depressive Disorder, Recurrent
	295.70	Schizoaffective Disorder
	310.1	Personality Change Due to . . . [Indicate the General Medical Condition]
	V62.82	Bereavement
	_____	_____
	_____	_____

EMPLOYMENT DISCRIMINATION

BEHAVIORAL DEFINITIONS

1. Experience of discrimination by coworkers and/or supervisor due to sexual orientation.
2. Sexual harassment experienced at work.
3. Loss of employment due to sexual orientation.
4. Subjective experience of hopelessness, frustration and/or victimization.
5. Difficulty concentrating and completing work-related tasks.
6. Pressure from coworkers to disclose facts about personal life.
7. Recently passed up for a promotion due to employer/supervisor bias against gays/lesbians.
8. Disclosure of gay/lesbian sexual orientation to coworkers.
9. Employment termination because of HIV status.
10. Conflicts in primary relationship because of employer policies and/or practices (e.g., lack of domestic partner benefits, no discrimination policies).
11. Uncomfortable about taking same sex partner to work-related social functions (e.g., holiday party, company picnic).

___. _____
  _____
___. _____
  _____
___. _____
  _____

LONG-TERM GOALS

1. Reduction of negative feelings (e.g., hopelessness, frustration) associated with employment.

2. Elimination of harassment experienced at work.
3. Development of effective coping skills to deal with incidents of discrimination at work.
4. Attainment of new employment.
5. Decision to seek other employment.
6. Increased level of support by employer.

—. _____
   _____
—. _____
   _____
—. _____
   _____

SHORT-TERM OBJECTIVES

1. Openly discuss problems occurring at work. (1)

2. Verbalize emotional reactions to any workplace discrimination. (2)

3. Identify possible solutions to problem at work. (3)

4. Verbalize the impact that work problem has had on relationship with partner. (4, 5)

5. Identify coworkers who are supportive of gay men and/or lesbians. (6, 7)

6. Enlist help of coworkers who are supportive. (8)

7. Verbalize an understanding of laws, or workplace policies, that prohibit discrimination based on sexual orientation and/or HIV status. (9, 10, 11, 12)

8. Consult with attorney regarding legal rights related to em-

THERAPEUTIC INTERVENTIONS

1. Assess client's problem, including primary complaint regarding employment discrimination, history of similar concerns, and any steps taken to resolve conflicts.

2. Use active listening skills (e.g., paraphrasing, emotional reflection) to establish trust with client and encourage honest self-disclosure of emotions related to work issues.

3. Using solution-focused method as client "miracle question" (e.g., If you woke up tomorrow and the problem was gone how, would you know? What changes would have happened?) and encourage client to begin to work toward self-generated solutions.

4. Inquire as to impact employment conflicts have had on couple.

ployment discrimination or harassment. (11, 12)

9. Identify resources available to assist with employment conflict resolution. (13, 14)

10. Read books on lesbian and gay men in the workplace. (15)

11. Demonstrate new coping skills (e.g., asking offending person to stop, informing person of consequences of further harassment, informing supervisor) to deal with problem at work. (16, 17)

12. List pros and cons of staying in current job and/or field. (18)

13. Decide whether or not to stay in job and/or field. (19)

14. Develop a plan to terminate job. (20)

15. Identify other occupations which might be of interest and more supportive of gays/lesbians. (21, 22, 23)

16. Participate in job training to learn new skills. (24)

17. Consult with job coach to assist in developing job search strategy. (25)

18. Actively seek new employment. (26)

___. _____
_____

___. _____
_____

___. _____
_____

5. Arrange conjoint sessions with partner to facilitate discussion of impact of job problem on couple. (See Intimate Partner Conflicts chapter of this *Planner*.)

6. Assist client in identifying coworkers who are supportive. Ask him/her to casually bring up social conversations about gay/lesbian topics in the news to "test the water."

7. Probe client about any coworkers who are openly lesbian/gay at work.

8. Encourage client to share his/her concerns with supportive coworkers and enlist their support.

9. Provide client with basic information regarding work place laws against discrimination based on sexual orientation and/or HIV.

10. Assign client homework of talking to human resources department to inquire about nondiscrimination policies and grievance procedures.

11. Refer to an attorney specializing in work place discrimination.

12. Refer client to gay chapter of American Civil Liberties Union.

13. Educate client as to resources available to assist in conflict resolution (e.g., Human Rights Campaign Fund, employer's human resources department,

outside mediation service, attorney, union, State Labor Board).

14. Assign client homework of listing all possible resources to assist in resolving conflict; process list and solicit commitment from client to make contact with one or more resources for support.

15. Assign client homework of reading books on lesbian and gay men in the workplace [e.g., *Straight Jobs, Gay Lives* (Friskopp & Silverstein); *Cracking the Corporate Closet: The 200 Best (and Worst) Companies to Work For* (Baker, Obrien, & Henning); *Out in the Workplace: Gay and Lesbian Professionals Tell Their Stories* (Rasi & Rodriguez-Nogues)].

16. Teach client assertiveness skills and practice their use in session.

17. Role play with client offensive interactions from work and have client practice new assertive ways of dealing with situation. Process emotional reactions to exercise in session.

18. Have client list pros and cons of staying in current job and/or field.

19. Assist client in processing thoughts and feelings and then in deciding whether or not to stay in present job and/or field.

20. Assist client in developing plan to terminate job, specifying

when notice will be given, job search strategies, and economic plan to deal with unemployment.

21. Assess client's work history and skills.

22. Perform psychological testing (e.g., Strong-Campbell, 16PF, WAIS-R) to assist client in determining jobs that suit personality, interests, and abilities.

23. Assign client to read *What Color Is Your Parachute?* (Bolles). Process reaction in session.

24. Refer to community-based job training (e.g., vocational rehabilitation, community college).

25. Refer to job coach who can provide assistance with resume writing, job search, and so on.

26. Monitor client's progress regarding job search. Provide positive reinforcement for all efforts and discuss any obstacles/setbacks.

___. _____

_____

___. _____

_____

___. _____

_____

DIAGNOSTIC SUGGESTIONS

Axis I:

296.xx	Major Depressive Disorder
300.00	Anxiety Disorder, NOS
300.4	Dysthymic Disorder
309.0	Adjustment Disorder with Depressed Mood
309.2	Adjustment Disorder with Anxiety
V62.2	Occupational Problem
_____	_____
_____	_____

FAMILY OF ORIGIN CONFLICTS

BEHAVIORAL DEFINITIONS

1. Frequent conflict (e.g., arguing, yelling) with parents and/or siblings about sexual orientation.
2. Family members have ceased contact with client because of client's sexual orientation.
3. Extended periods of time with very little communication with parents and/or siblings.
4. Self report of loneliness, hurt, and abandonment because of family's rejection.
5. Partner accused by family of "turning" client gay.
6. Hiding of gay/lesbian orientation from family due to fear of rejection.
7. Family member hiding client's sexual orientation from other family members.

—. _____
   _____
—. _____
   _____
—. _____
   _____

LONG-TERM GOALS

1. Decrease in conflict with parents and/or siblings about sexual orientation.
2. Increase in comfortable contact with family members.
3. Acceptance by family of son's or daughter's sexual orientation.
4. Acceptance by family members of son's or daughter's same sex partner.

5. Decrease in fear of rejection associated with living "out" as a gay or lesbian.

—. _____

_____

—. _____

_____

—. _____

_____

SHORT-TERM OBJECTIVES

1. Express feelings (e.g., anger, disappointment, sadness) about conflict with family openly and honestly. (1)

2. Define the nature of the conflict with family. (2)

3. List the ways personal behavior has contributed to or exacerbated the conflict. (3)

4. Verbalize an understanding of how family dynamics play a role in perpetuating the conflict. (4, 5, 6)

5. List advantages and disadvantages of maintaining contact with family and/or disclosing sexual orientation to them. (7)

6. Write a plan to disclose sexual orientation to family. (8)

7. Role play disclosure of sexual orientation to family in session. (9)

8. Disclose sexual orientation to family according to written plan. (10)

THERAPEUTIC INTERVENTIONS

1. Actively build trust with client to facilitate open communication of feelings associated with family conflict.

2. Assess the nature of the problem and assist the client in more precisely identifying the conflict.

3. Assist client in identifying how his/her behavior (e.g., hiding sexual orientation, taking a militant stand about homosexuality, dismissing parents' feelings) has contributed to or exacerbated the conflict.

4. Explore with the client regarding family interactions, roles, control issues, belief systems, alliances, degree of closeness in various relationships, and so on.

5. Educate the client about family dynamics and assist him/her in understanding how these have contributed to conflict.

6. Have client draw a genogram detailing roles within the

9. Family members attend and actively participate in therapy sessions. (11)

10. Demonstrate increased communication skills in session. (12, 13, 14)

11. Client and family express feelings related to conflict in session. (14, 15, 16)

12. Family members verbalize emotions (disappointment, guilt, shame, etc.) about client being lesbian/gay. (15, 16)

13. Family members verbalize an increased understanding of homosexuality. (17, 18)

14. Family members read books about homosexuality and its impact on families. (18)

15. Family attend a support group. (19)

16. Family members identify any religious beliefs that contribute to conflict and/or lack of acceptance of client's sexual orientation. (20)

17. Family consult with religious leaders to discuss questions about client's sexual orientation. (21)

18. Family members will identify 10 myths or personally held beliefs about homosexuals and replace them with more realistic, positive beliefs. (22)

19. Express emotional reactions to the fact that partner is not being included in family activities. (23, 24)

family and other conflicts between members. Process with therapist in session.

7. Assign client to list advantages (e.g., being more honest, staying connected) and disadvantages (e.g., family may disown client, family is unwilling to support client emotionally) of maintaining contact with and/or disclosing sexual orientation to family.

8. Assign client to write a detailed plan of how to disclose sexual orientation to family (e.g., who is to be told, where, what) and process this plan and its ramifications in sessions.

9. Have client role play disclosure of his/her sexual orientation to family in session. Ask client several pointed questions about sexual orientation (e.g., Did we make you gay? Do you want to be the opposite sex? Do you have AIDS?) that are likely to be asked so client is prepared to deal with family with minimal amounts of anxiety.

10. Have client disclose sexual orientation to family according to plan. Process reactions in session. (See Sexual Identity Confusion chapter in this *Planner*.)

11. Encourage family to attend sessions to facilitate conflict resolution.

12. Teach family and client positive communication skills (e.g., "I" messages, active listening, no interrupting, reflection of

20. Family will verbalize an understanding of how to be supportive of client and how current behavior has negatively impacted relationship. (25)

21. Family and client plan activities together. (26)

22. Family and client report increased level of social activities outside of session. (27)

___. _____
_____
___. _____
_____
___. _____
_____

feelings). Monitor for their use in session and provide positive reinforcement.

13. Provide assertiveness training to client and family.

14. Encourage client and family members to express emotional reactions to conflict.

15. Probe family members about negative emotions regarding client's sexual orientation.

16. Process family members' grief (e.g., not having grand children, no son-in-law or daughter-in-law) related to client's sexual orientation.

17. Educate family about homosexuality.

18. Assign family books on homosexuality (e.g., *Is It a Choice?* [Marcus], *Now That You Know: What Every Parent Should Know About Homosexuality* [Fairchild & Hayward], *Beyond Acceptance: Parents of Lesbians and Gays Talk About Their Experience* [Griffin, Wirth, & Wirth], *The Family Heart: A Memoir of When Our Son Came Out* [Dew], and *Loving Someone Gay* [Clark]). Process key points with therapist in session.

19. Refer family to support groups (e.g., Parents and Friends of Lesbians and Gays).

20. Probe family about any religious beliefs that may be contributing to conflict with client.

21. Refer family to religious leaders of same denomination that are supportive of gays/lesbians. (See Religious Conflicts chapter in this *Planner.*)

22. Assign family homework to list 10 personally held beliefs or myths (e.g., gay men and lesbians are mentally ill, homosexuality is caused by faulty parenting, homosexuals are child molesters) and assist them in replacing them with more positive, realistic beliefs.

23. Encourage client to express emotional reactions to partner being excluded from family activities.

24. Have client make a request for change using assertiveness training model (e.g., "When you _____ , I feel _____ , and I would like you to _____ .").

25. Explore with family ways that their current behavior has negatively impacted relationship with client. Press for commitment to change.

26. Encourage and assist client and family in planning activities together. Discuss plans in session.

27. Provide positive feedback about increased social contact with family and process any new conflicts.

—. _____
    _____
—. _____
    _____
—. _____
    _____

DIAGNOSTIC SUGGESTIONS

Axis I:	300.02	Generalized Anxiety Disorder
	300.00	Anxiety Disorder NOS
	309.24	Adjustment Disorder with Anxiety
	296.2	Major Depressive Disorder, Single Episode
	296.3	Major Depressive Disorder, Recurrent
	302.85	Gender Identity Disorder in Adolescents or Adults
	300.4	Dysthymic Disorder
	309.0	Adjustment Disorder with Depressed Mood
	309.28	Adjustment Disorder with Mixed Anxiety and Depressed Mood
	313.82	Identity Problem
	V61.20	Parent-Child Relational Problem
	V61.8	Sibling Relational Problem
	_____	_____
	_____	_____

FEMALE SEXUAL DYSFUNCTION

BEHAVIORAL DEFINITIONS

1. No sexual activity within the couple for over six months.
2. Little or no desire for sexual activity.
3. Subjective sense of discomfort and/or anxiety during sexual activities.
4. Recurrent lack of usual physiological response of sexual excitement and arousal (genital lubrication and swelling).
5. Preoccupation with orgasm as a goal of sexual activity.
6. Dissatisfaction with the inability to achieve an orgasm during the couple's sexual activities.
7. Genital pain before, during, or after sexual activity.
8. Disagreement within the couple about the ideal frequency and/or type of sexual activities.

—. _____
   _____
—. _____
   _____
   _____
—. _____
   _____

LONG-TERM GOALS

1. Reduce homophobic, sexist, and negative beliefs about sexuality that have contributed to avoiding and/or ceasing sexual activities.
2. Increase the frequency, range of, and satisfaction with sexual activity within the couple.
3. Increase desire for and enjoyment of sexual activity.
4. Increase ability to reach orgasm without and/or with partner.
5. Eliminate pain and promote subjective pleasure before, during, and after sexual activity.

6. Engage in a range of mutually agreed upon sexual activities which are a source of pleasure.

—. _____
_____

—. _____
_____

—. _____
_____

SHORT-TERM OBJECTIVES

1. Commit to attend and participate in conjoint sessions with partner. (1)

2. Identify sexual problem and treatment goals in behavioral terms. (2, 3)

3. Identify current sexual roles and practices. (4)

4. Identify and clarify relationship conflicts. (5)

5. Verbalize an understanding of the impact of relationship conflicts upon sexual activities. (6)

6. List any conflicts outside the relationship that may be affecting sexual functioning. (7)

7. Describe childhood experiences that have contributed to feelings of anxiety, fear, and shame about sexuality. (8, 9, 10, 14)

8. Describe sexual history of each partner and the couple. (11, 12)

9. List negative messages about sexuality and homosexuality learned from previous/current

THERAPEUTIC INTERVENTIONS

1. Educate client(s) about the need for both partners to participate in sexual counseling and press for commitment for both members to attend and participate.

2. Assist the client(s) in describing sexual problem and treatment goals in behavioral terms (e.g., both partners dissatisfied with sex once a month and want to increase it to once a week, partner would like to be able to achieve orgasm during couple's sexual activities).

3. Assign client(s) homework that asks each partner to write a description of how their relationship will be different after the problem is resolved. Have partners read to each other in session.

4. Inquire as to current sexual roles and activities (e.g., who initiates sex, which activities are performed by whom).

5. Probe about conflicts and disagreements within the couple.

religious experiences (e.g., Sunday School, temple, confirmation, preparation for Bat Mitzvah). (13)

10. Identify any sexual abuse history. (14)

11. Verbalize an understanding of the impact of childhood sexual abuse upon current sexual problems. (15)

12. Verbalize the situations and behaviors needed for each partner to feel safe during sexual activity. (16)

13. Verbalize an understanding of how internalized homophobia contributes to fear, shame, and anxiety during sex. (17)

14. Identify automatic thoughts that increase anxiety, fear, and shame during sexual activities. (18)

15. Replace negative, dysfunctional cognitions with positive, reality-based thoughts. (19)

16. Describe how negative body image has inhibited sexual pleasure. (20, 21)

17. Verbalize an understanding of how sexism and sexual objectification have contributed to negative body image. (20, 21)

18. Complete a list of 10 anxiety/guilt provoking sexual activities. (22)

19. Practice deep muscle relaxation techniques. (23)

20. Practice desensitization exercises using deep muscle

6. Assist client(s) in understanding connection between relationship conflicts and sexual dissatisfaction.

7. Assign each partner to list areas of conflict outside of relationship (e.g., work, family). Educate couple on how these conflicts may be affecting sexual functioning.

8. Encourage client(s) to describe their childhood experiences that have contributed to feelings of anxiety, fear and shame with emphasis upon sexual messages within family of origin.

9. Ask each partner to describe where, what, and when they learned about homosexuality.

10. Explore role of family of origin in teaching negative attitudes regarding sexuality, homosexuality, and women.

11. Inquire about the sexual history of couple, including previous activities enjoyed, frequency, and how activities were negotiated within the couple.

12. Ask each partner to describe her sexual history prior to this relationship focusing upon information, attitudes, and emotions about sexuality in general and homosexuality specifically.

13. Assign clients to list negative messages learned about sexuality and homosexuality in previous/current religious experiences. (See Religious

relaxation and anxiety/guilt hierarchy. (24)

21. Read and discuss books assigned on women's/lesbian sexuality. (25)

22. Abstain from substance abuse patterns that interfere with sexual response. (26)

23. Identify any physical problems or medications that may be affecting sexual functioning. (27, 28)

24. Cooperate with a physician's complete examination and report results. (28)

25. Describe any signs and symptoms of depression. (29)

26. Verbalize an understanding of the impact of depression upon sexual problem(s). (29, 30)

27. Identify and participate in a strategy to alleviate depression. (30)

28. Discuss feelings surrounding infidelity and make commitment to fidelity agreement. (31)

29. Practice saying no to sexual activities which are not desired and/or anxiety-provoking. (32)

30. Identify and experiment with sexual aids that may increase pleasure. (33)

31. Verbalize how focusing upon orgasm as a goal has affected sexual pleasure. (34)

Conflicts chapter in this *Planner*.)

14. Explore clients' history for experience of sexual trauma or abuse.

15. Educate client(s) about the impact of childhood sexual abuse upon sexual problems. (See Sexual Abuse chapter in this *Planner*.)

16. Using a solution-focused approach, ask each partner to identify what they need to feel safe before, during, and after sexual activity. Encourage partners to establish these solutions.

17. Probe client(s) for homophobic beliefs and educate about the impact upon sexual pleasure. Assist client(s) in developing positive beliefs. (See Internalized Homophobia chapter in this *Planner*.)

18. Educate clients about the nature of automatic thoughts and ask them to describe what comes to mind before, during, and after sexual activity.

19. Assist client(s) in challenging negative automatic thoughts and replace them with positive, reality-based thoughts.

20. Educate client(s) about the negative effects of sexual objectification on body image and sexual pleasure.

21. Assign client(s) to read *The Beauty Myth* (Wolf). Process key ideas with therapist.

32. Practice sensate focus exercises. (35, 36, 37, 38)

33. Write a journal of sexual fantasies, beliefs, and attitudes that stimulate sexual arousal. (39)

34. Verbalize an undesrtanding of the partner's sexual preferences. (37, 39, 40)

35. Communicate sexual desires to partner. (37, 40, 41)

36. List sexual activities which the couple has mutually agreed to explore. (41)

37. Experiment with new mutually agreed-upon sexual activities and settings. (42)

38. Identify sexual activities that are mutually satisfying and stimulating. (43)

39. Report increase in overall sexual activity, satisfaction, and pleasure within the couple. (44)

—. _____

_____

—. _____

_____

—. _____

_____

22. Assign the development of a hierarchy listing ten activities (e.g., being nude with partner, having oral sex) that provoke anxiety and/or guilt emotions on a scale of 1 to 10.

23. Teach client(s) deep muscle relaxation techniques.

24. Assign client(s) graduated de-sensitization exercises using anxiety/guilt hierarchy and deep muscle relaxation techniques. Have client(s) start with the least anxiety/guilt provoking activities and move up the hierarchy as negative emotions decrease to tolerable levels.

25. Assign books [e.g., *Lesbian Sex* (Loulan), *The New Our Bodies, Ourselves* (The Boston Women's Health Collective), or *Shared Intimacies* (Barbach & Levine)] that provide accurate sexual information about women's health and sexuality.

26. Educate client(s) about the impact of substance abuse upon sexuality and press for agreement for abstinence.

27. Review medications taken by client(s) with regard to their possible negative side effects on sexual functioning.

28. Refer to a Women's Health Center or lesbian-friendly physician for a complete physical to rule out any organic basis for dysfunction.

29. Assess for depression and educate client(s) about the impact

of depression upon sexual functioning.

30. Assist client(s) in developing strategies to deal with depression including individual psychotherapy and/or referral to a medical professional for prescription of antidepressants. (See Depression chapter in this *Planner.*)

31. Review any sexual relationships outside the couple's fidelity contract; discuss its impact upon the couple's sexual relationship. (See Intimate Relationship Conflicts chapter in this *Planner.*)

32. Encourage client(s) to assertively refuse any sexual activities which are not desired and/ or anxiety-provoking.

33. Educate client(s) about the use of sexual aids (e.g., lesbian erotica, vibrators, lotions) that may increase sexual pleasure.

34. Educate client(s) about the continuum of sexual pleasure and the negative effects of focusing on orgasm as a goal.

35. Assign initial sensate focus homework, asking couple to provide one another gentle touch and massage that avoids genital stimulation.

36. Assign client(s) to alternate stimulating each other's genitals but proscribe orgasm. Encourage partner who is being stimulated to direct the speed and intensity of the stimulation.

37. Assign client(s) to demonstrate satisfying masturbation to one another. Process reactions to assignment in session.

38. Explore reactions to sensate focus exercises and assist client(s) in identifying any sources of conflict.

39. Assign client(s) to keep a journal of sexual fantasies, feelings, and thoughts.

40. Ask client(s) to describe sexual fantasies, feelings, and thoughts from journal and discuss which are mutually stimulating and interesting.

41. Ask client(s) to decide which sexual activities they would like to explore. Process any disagreement.

42. Assign couple(s) to begin experimenting with new sexual activities. Process reactions, success, and failure with therapist in session.

43. Ask client(s) to identify which activities are a source of pleasure and encourage them to continue to participate in them.

44. Inquire as to how often the couple is engaging in sexual activity and reinforce progress.

—. _____

_____

—. _____

_____

—. _____

_____

DIAGNOSTIC SUGGESTIONS

Axis I:

	302.71	Hypoactive Sexual Desire Disorder
	302.79	Sexual Aversion Disorder
	302.72	Female Sexual Arousal Disorder
	302.73	Female Orgasmic Disorder
	302.76	Dyspareunia [Not Due to a General Medical Condition]
	306.51	Vaginismus [Not Due to a General Medical Condition]
	V61.1	Partner Relational Problem
	625.8	Female Hypoactive Sexual Desire Disorder Due to . . . [Indicate the General Medical Condition]
	625.0	Female Dyspareunia Due to . . . [Indicate the General Medical Condition]
	302.9	Sexual Disorder NOS
_____	_____	
_____	_____	

GRIEF/MULTIPLE LOSS

BEHAVIORAL DEFINITIONS

1. Thoughts dominated by loss coupled with poor concentration, tearful spells, and confusion about the future.
2. Multiple losses of friends, partners, and acquaintances to AIDS that led to depression and discouragement.
3. Avoidance of people with HIV/AIDS.
4. Strong emotional response exhibited when losses are discussed.
5. Lack of appetite, weight loss, and/or insomnia as well as other depression signs that began after the loss.
6. Feelings of guilt that not enough was done for the lost significant other or an unreasonable belief of having contributed to the death of significant other.
7. Avoidance of talking on anything more than a superficial level about the loss.
8. Loss of a social support system due to multiple losses.

__. _____
   _____
__. _____
   _____
   _____
__. _____
   _____

LONG-TERM GOALS

1. Begin a healthy grieving process around the loss.
2. Develop an awareness of how the avoidance of grieving has affected life and begin the healing process.
3. Complete the process of letting go of the lost significant other.

4. Resolve the loss and begin renewing old relationships and initiating new contacts with others.
5. Rebuild social support system so it is adequate to meet emotional needs.

—. _____
   _____
—. _____
   _____
—. _____
   _____

SHORT-TERM OBJECTIVES

1. Identify the losses that have been experienced in life. (1, 2, 3)

2. Verbalize an increased understanding of the steps in the grief process. (4, 5, 6, 7)

3. Identify what stages of grief have been experienced in the continuum of the grieving process. (5)

4. Identify how social support has been impacted by multiple losses. (6)

5. Read books on the topic of grief in the gay/lesbian community to increase knowledge of the experience, validate the feelings associated with loss, and increase a sense of hope. (7)

6. Tell the detailed story of the current loss and its impact on daily life. (2, 3, 8, 9)

THERAPEUTIC INTERVENTIONS

1. Actively build the level of trust with the client in individual sessions through consistent eye contact, active listening, unconditional positive regard and warm acceptance to help increase his/her ability to identify and express thoughts and feelings.

2. Explore with client the losses that have been experienced.

3. Ask client to elaborate in an autobiography on the circumstances, feelings, and effects of the loss or losses in life.

4. Ask client to talk to several people about losses in their lives as to how they felt and coped. Process findings.

5. Educate the client on the stages of the grieving process and answer any questions.

6. Assist client with drawing an Eco-Map detailing social support network before and after

7. Begin verbalizing feelings associated with the loss. (8, 9, 10)

8. Identify how HIV status has affected grief process. (11)

9. Watch videos on the theme of grief and loss to compare personal experience with characters in the film. (12)

10. Attend a grief support group. (13)

11. Identify how avoiding dealing with the loss has negatively impacted life. (6, 14)

12. Identify how the use of substances has aided the avoidance of feelings associated with the loss. (15, 16)

13. Agree to treatment that focuses on substance abuse which has been used to escape from the pain of grief. (16)

14. Verbalize and resolve feelings of anger or guilt focused on self or deceased loved one(s) that blocks the grieving process. (10, 17, 18, 19)

15. Write letters to lost loved one(s) to express memories and feelings associated with the loss. (19, 20)

16. Acknowledge dependency on lost loved one(s) and begin to refocus life on independent actions to meet emotional needs. (6, 17, 19, 21)

multiple losses and process with therapist.

7. Ask client to read the books *In the Shadow of the Epidemic* (Odets), *AIDS: The Ultimate Challenge* (Kubler-Ross), *Gay Widowers: Life after the Death of a Partner* (Shernoff & Picano), *Borrowed Time: An AIDS Memoir* (Monette), or another book on grief and loss in the gay/lesbian community.

8. Assign client to keep a daily grief journal to be shared in therapy sessions.

9. Ask client to bring pictures or mementos connected with the loss to a session and talk about them with therapist.

10. Assist client in identifying and expressing feelings connected with the loss.

11. Assist client in identifying how his/her HIV status (e.g., survivor guilt for HIV negative clients, concerns about mortality for HIV positive clients) has affected the grieving process. (See HIV/AIDS chapter in this *Planner*.)

12. Ask client to watch the films "Long Time Companion," "Common Threads" or similar film that focuses on loss and grieving in gay/lesbian community and then discuss how characters cope with loss and express their grief.

17. Identify causes for feelings of regret associated with actions toward or relationship with the deceased. (22)

18. Express thoughts and feelings about deceased that went unexpressed while deceased was alive. (19, 20, 23, 24)

19. Identify the positive characteristics of the deceased loved one(s), the positive aspects of the relationship with the deceased loved one(s), and how these things may be remembered. (25, 26)

20. Identify and participate in a ritual which commemorates the loss(es). (26)

21. Decrease statements and feelings of being responsible for the loss. (17, 18, 27)

22. Decrease time spent daily focused on the loss. (28)

23. Attend and participate in a network therapy session (composed of people in client's life who have experienced the same loss) focused on each member sharing his/her experience with grief. (29)

24. Implement acts of spiritual faith as a source of comfort and hope. (30)

—. _____
   _____
—. _____
   _____
—. _____
   _____

13. Ask client to attend a grief/loss support group and report to therapist how he/she felt about attending.

14. Ask client to list ways avoidance of grieving has negatively impacted his/her life.

15. Assess the role of substance abuse as an escape from the pain of grief.

16. Arrange for chemical dependence treatment so grief issues can be faced while client is clean and sober. (See Chemical Dependence chapter in this _Planner_.)

17. Explore feelings of anger, abandonment, or guilt that surround the loss, helping client understand the sources for such feelings.

18. Encourage client to forgive self and/or deceased to resolve feelings of guilt or anger.

19. Ask client to write a letter to lost person describing fond memories, painful and regretful memories, and how he/she currently feels. Read the letter in session.

20. Assign client to write to the deceased loved one(s) with a special focus on feelings associated with the last meaningful contact with the person.

21. Assist client in identifying how he/she depended upon significant other, expressing and resolving the accompanying

feelings of abandonment and being left alone.

22. Assign client to make a list of all the regrets he/she has concerning the loss and to process list with therapist.

23. Conduct an "empty chair" exercise with the client where he/she focuses on expressing to lost loved one(s) imagined in the empty chair what he/she never said while that loved one was present.

24. Assign client to visit the grave of loved one(s) to "talk to" deceased and ventilate feelings.

25. Ask client to list the most positive aspects of and memories about the relationship with the lost loved one(s).

26. Assist client in identifying rituals which commemorate the loss(es), such as sewing a panel for the AIDS quilt, visiting the grave site, participating in AIDS candlelight vigils, and so on, and encourage his/her participation.

27. Use a Rational Emotive Therapy approach to confront client statements of responsibility for the loss and compare them to reality-based facts.

28. Suggest that the client set aside a specific time-limited period each day to focus on mourning the loss. After time period is up the client will get on with regular daily activities with agreement to put off thoughts until next scheduled time.

(Mourning times could include putting on dark clothing and/or sad music and so on. Clothing would be changed when allotted time is up.)

29. Conduct a group session with the client participating where each member talks about his/her experience related to the loss.

30. Assess client's beliefs and encourage him/her to rely upon his/her spiritual faith and activities (e.g., prayer, meditation, worship, music), and fellowship as sources of support if appropriate.

—. _____
   _____
—. _____
   _____
—. _____
   _____

DIAGNOSTIC SUGGESTIONS

Axis I:	296.2x	Major Depressive Disorder, Single Episode
	296.3x	Major Depressive Disorder, Recurrent
	V62.82	Bereavement
	309.0	Adjustment Disorder with Depressed Mood
	309.3	Adjustment Disorder with Disturbance of Conduct
	300.4	Dysthymic Disorder
	_____	_____
	_____	_____

HATE CRIME VICTIM

BEHAVIORAL DEFINITIONS

1. Confirmed self-report or account by others of physical assault (e.g., beating, stabbing, hitting) by stranger because of sexual orientation.
2. Self-report of being forced to engage in sexual activity (e.g., vaginal intercourse, fellatio, anal intercourse) with another person.
3. Bruises, cuts, or abrasions that give evidence of assault.
4. Recurrent, intrusive, and disturbing thoughts, dreams, and memories of assault.
5. Blaming victimization on characteristics of self (e.g., being gay/lesbian, weak, "flamboyant").
6. Restricted range of affect.
7. Pronounced disturbance of mood and affect (e.g., frequent and prolonged periods of depression, irritability, anxiety, and/or apathetic withdrawal).
8. Avoidance of social activities (e.g., work, activities with friends and/or family).
9. Subjective sense of numbing, detaching, or absence of emotional responsiveness.
10. Avoidance of people and activities that are reminders of the assault.
11. Difficulty sleeping, poor concentration, motor restlessness.

___. _____
_____
___. _____
_____
___. _____
_____

LONG-TERM GOALS

1. Eliminate intrusive thoughts, nightmares, and memories of assault.
2. Place responsibility for assault on the assailant.
3. Resume social activities.
4. Increase feelings of confidence and satisfaction with gay/lesbian identity.
5. Return to the level of emotional and social functioning present before the assault.

—. _____
_____
—. _____
_____
—. _____
_____

SHORT-TERM OBJECTIVES

1. Give an accurate and emotionally honest description of the assault. (1, 2, 3, 4)

2. Identify and express the guilt, shame, anger, helplessness, and/or self-blame associated with the assault. (4)

3. Comply with a comprehensive physical evaluation to assure that no serious injuries have been sustained and/or are untreated. (5)

4. Report results from physical examination and pursue any medical treatment necessary to recover from the assault. (6)

5. Cooperate with assessment for suicidality and depression. (7)

6. Verbalize how assault has impacted functioning in social,

THERAPEUTIC INTERVENTIONS

1. Actively build the level of trust with the client in individual sessions through consistent eye contact, active listening, unconditional positive regard, and warm acceptance to help increase his/her ability to identify and express feelings.

2. Gather a history of assault including time of day, location, number of assailants, and descriptions of any police involvement (report at station, response of officers, etc.).

3. Encourage and support the client in verbally expressing and clarifying his/her perception of the facts associated with the assault.

4. Explore client's feelings associated with the assault

work, and family situations. (8, 9)

7. Cooperate with standardized psychological testing to determine severity of trauma's emotional and behavioral impact. (9)

8. Read books regarding lesbian/gay victims of violent crime to increase awareness of, and recovery from, traumatic experiences. (10)

9. Attend victim support groups that are sensitive to gay/lesbian victims of assault. (11)

10. Verbalize an understanding of the psychological impact of trauma. (10, 11, 12)

11. Identify any pattern of blaming self for the assault. (13)

12. Terminate self-blame for the abuse and place responsibility on the perpetrator. (14)

13. Verbalize an understanding of how societal homophobia and the perpetrator's own background of hate created climate for victimization, not being gay/lesbian. (15, 16)

14. Challenge negative self-talk and replace with more realistic beliefs. (17, 18)

15. Attend self-defense classes to decrease feelings of helplessness and fear. (19)

16. Describe any conflicts with partner, friends, and/or family that started or increased since assault (e.g., viewing the vic-

including those of guilt, shame, anger, helplessness, and/or self-blame.

5. Refer client to physician for a physical exam.

6. Inquire as to results of physical examination and encourage client to follow-through with physician's recommendations for medical care.

7. Assess client for signs and symptoms of depression and suicidality; referring to psychiatrist for medications if indicated. (See Depression chapter in this *Planner*.)

8. Assist client in identifying the negative impact that the assault has had on his/her functioning at work and in social or family interactions.

9. Administer the *Clinician-Administered PTSD Scale* (CAPS; Blake et al.), and/or the *PTSD Symptom Scale* (PSS; Foa et al.), to assist with diagnosis and to determine the severity of symptoms and impairment.

10. Suggest the client read books about gay/lesbian victims of violent crimes [e.g., *Hate Crimes* (Herek)].

11. Refer client to support groups (victims of violent crimes, rape, etc.) that are sensitive to gays/lesbians; encourage and reinforce attendance.

12. Educate client about common reactions to assault (e.g., anxiety, flashbacks, avoidance).

tim as weak, blaming the victim for the assault). (20)

17. Identify those friends and family members who are understanding and supportive. (20, 21)

18. List the advantages and disadvantages of reporting and prosecuting the crime. (22)

19. Verbalize an understanding of legal resources in the community that are sensitive to gay/lesbian victims of crime. (23)

20. Practice slow, deep breathing to decrease anxiety. (24)

21. Demonstrate the ability to quantify distress by using Subjective Units of Distress (SUDs). (25)

22. List situations, places, and people that are being avoided. (26, 27)

23. Arrange the avoided situations into an anxiety hierarchy. (28)

24. Practice imaginal systematic desensitization exposure to anxiety-producing elements of the assault to reduce fear and avoidance. (29, 30)

25. Significant others verbalize understanding of and support for client(s). (31)

26. Confront avoided situations with a supportive friend, partner, or family member. (30, 31, 32)

13. Explore for the existence of self-blame for the victimization.

14. Confront client regarding self-blame and assist client in placing responsibility for victimization on the perpetrator.

15. Educate client about the nature, incidence, and severity of homophobia-related crimes.

16. Assign client homework of contacting the Gay and Lesbian Alliance Against Defamation (GLAAD) either through a local chapter or their web site to inquire about the problems of hate crimes against gays/lesbians. Process reactions in session.

17. Educate client about recording automatic thoughts (e.g., "I was attacked because I am too effeminate/masculine") to identify negative self-talk.

18. Assist client in replacing distorted, unrealistic self-talk with realistic self-talk (e.g., "I was attacked because the assailant was virulently homophobic") that does not blame self for assault.

19. Refer to self-defense classes to increase client's sense of control and empowerment.

20. Inquire about relationships with partner, friends, and family and assist client in identifying relationships that are sources of conflict and support. (See Intimate Relationship

27. Challenge any irrational fears about being re-victimized. (18, 33)

28. Participate in political/social activities which combat crime and victimization of gays/ lesbians to increase sense of efficacy over victimization. (34)

29. Resume previous level of social activities. (35)

—. _____
   _____
—. _____
   _____
—. _____
   _____

Conflict chapter in this *Planner*.)

21. Assist client in identifying friends and/or family that would be supportive of client and encourage client to seek their support.

22. Ask client to list the advantages (e.g., offender may be found and prosecuted, client will feel more in control) and disadvantages (reporting the crime may force the client out of the closet, police may be insensitive to victim's needs) of reporting and prosecuting the crime.

23. Educate client about appropriate legal resources (e.g., victim witness programs, district attorney, legal aid, and legal assistance from local gay/lesbian community services center) that are available to and understanding of victims of gay/ lesbian hate crimes.

24. Train the client in deep, abdominal breathing techniques to decrease anxiety and encourage their practice in and between sessions.

25. Educate client about the use of SUDs to rate the degree of anxiety experienced generally or in the presence of specific stimuli.

26. Provide client with examples of situations (e.g., going out at night, returning to site of the assault, being in the dark at home) that are commonly

avoided as a result of being physically attacked.

27. Ask client to list situations that he/she is avoiding due to the assault.

28. Assist client in creating a hierarchy by his/her rating avoided situations on a scale of 1 to 100 subjective units of discomfort.

29. Conduct imaginal systematic desensitization exposure using the hierarchy of avoided events (e.g., have client describe events/situations from the hierarchy of SUDs that have been decreased to tolerable or negligible levels).

30. Reinforce client's progress in reducing fear and avoidance by providing positive feedback and encouragement to the desensitization process.

31. Educate client's significant others about the effects of being victimized and *in vivo* exposure techniques. Enlist them in providing support as client confronts avoided situations.

32. Assign homework of *in vivo* exposure to anxiety-producing stimulus situations (e.g., being able to confront avoided situations with a friend, partner, family member). Process reactions with therapist in session.

33. Assist client in identifying irrational fears regarding being re-victimized and replacing those fears with more realistic beliefs regarding probabilities.

34. Refer client to political/social activities which combat crime and victimization of gays/lesbians (e.g., neighborhood watch programs, citizen patrols, and gay/lesbian political action groups).

35. Monitor client's progress toward increased social activity and positively reinforce movement toward that goal.

___. _____
_____
___. _____
_____
___. _____
_____

DIAGNOSTIC SUGGESTIONS

Axis I:	308.3	Acute Stress Disorder
	309.0	Adjustment Disorder with Depressed Mood
	309.24	Adjustment Disorder with Anxiety
	309.28	Adjustment Disorder with Mixed Anxiety and Depressed Mood
	300.12	Dissociative Amnesia
	300.4	Dysthymic Disorder
	296.xx	Major Depressive Disorder
	995.81	Physical Abuse of Adult (If Focus of Clinical Attention is on the Victim)
	309.81	Posttraumatic Stress Disorder
	995.81	Sexual Abuse of Adult (If Focus of Clinical Attention Is on the Victim)
	_____	_____
	_____	_____
Axis II:	301.83	Borderline Personality Disorder
	301.6	Dependent Personality Disorder
	301.50	Histrionic Personality Disorder
	_____	_____
	_____	_____

HOMOSEXUAL MARRIED TO HETEROSEXUAL

BEHAVIORAL DEFINITIONS

1. Disclosure of homosexuality to spouse.
2. Heterosexual spouse expression concern over possibility client may be homosexual.
3. "Coming out" to children.
4. Sense of isolation experienced by both spouses after disclosure of homosexuality.
5. Separation or divorce due to disclosure of homosexuality.
6. Conflict (e.g., anxiety, shame) over trying to live dual identities.
7. Feelings of betrayal, anger, and rage expressed by heterosexual spouse.
8. Feelings of loss associated with disclosure of homosexuality to heterosexual spouse.

___. _____
_____
___. _____
_____
___. _____
_____

LONG-TERM GOALS

1. Acceptance of homosexuality and its changes on the family and couple.
2. Disclosure of homosexuality to spouse and children.
3. Decrease level of denial utilized by family about client's sexual orientation.

4. Resolve feelings of betrayal, anger and rage associated with disclosure of homosexuality.
5. Increase awareness of the impact disclosure of homosexuality has on the family.
6. Resolve feelings associated with living as a married homosexual with dual identities.
7. Grieve losses experienced by the change in the marital relationship due to the disclosure of homosexuality.
8. Increase in social activities and a decrease in social isolation.
9. Acceptance of termination of the marital relationship.

—. _____
   _____
—. _____
   _____
—. _____
   _____

SHORT-TERM OBJECTIVES

1. Openly and honestly discuss coming to grips with homosexual identity and feelings associated with it. (1)

2. Heterosexual partner will describe reasons for suspecting spouse may be homosexual. (2)

3. Heterosexual spouse will verbalize the feelings associated with discovery of spouse's homosexuality (e.g., betrayal, rage, shock). (3, 4)

4. Heterosexual client will verbalize an understanding that spouse's homosexuality is not the result of any characteristic of the client (e.g., believing husband is gay because sex life has been dissatisfactory, or

THERAPEUTIC INTERVENTIONS

1. Actively build trust with client by demonstrating unconditional positive regard (e.g., summarizing, active listening).

2. Inquire as to reasons heterosexual client believes spouse may be homosexual.

3. Explore heterosexual client's emotional reactions to spouse's homosexuality and support by providing reassurance.

4. Journal conflicts and feelings about spouse's homosexuality and discuss in session with therapist.

5. Provide client(s) with basic information about homosexuality and redirect when heterosexual client takes responsibility for

wife is lesbian because client is not "man enough"). (5, 6)

5. Increase knowledge of homo-sexuality. (5, 6)

6. Read books on homosexuality and families. (6)

7. Speak directly to spouse about homosexual feelings, attractions, and experiences. (7, 8, 9)

8. Attend and actively participate in conjoint sessions. (10, 11, 12)

9. Discuss emotional impact of spouse disclosing homosexuality in session. (10, 11, 12)

10. List the pros and cons of maintaining the marriage. (13)

11. Couple will list options available to them now that spouse has "come-out." (14)

12. Each spouse will describe the emotional reactions to different relationship options available to them. (15)

13. Identify the emotional impact of each relationship option upon their children. (16)

14. Spouses will decide which option to choose regarding their relationship. (17)

15. Develop a plan for divorce which is mutually agreed upon. (18)

16. Verbalize the emotional reactions to termination of the relationship. (19)

17. Verbalize an understanding of the Campanaro-Cummings

orientation of homosexual spouse.

6. Assign clients to read books and publications on hetero-sexuals married to homosexuals (*The Other Side of the Closet* [Buxton], *Loving Someone Gay* [Clark]).

7. Discuss ways to approach sharing homosexual feelings, attractions, and experiences with spouse.

8. Encourage client to speak directly about personal experiences with homosexuality.

9. Assist client in decreasing anxiety about disclosing homosexuality to spouse by having her/him role play spouse while modeling assertive questioning and then switch roles. Process any emotional reactions to role play in session.

10. Facilitate conjoint sessions to assist spouses to speak clearly and empathically with one another about sexual orientation issues.

11. Support and assist client in session to disclose homosexuality to spouse.

12. Using role reversal technique, have each spouse switch places and discuss the problem and feelings from the other's perspective.

13. Assign homework of listing pros and cons of staying married.

stages of grieving experienced by a "heterosexual" spouse. (20)

18. Homosexual spouse will identify and participate in gay/lesbian resources in the community to bolster support. (21)

19. Identify community resources for social support. (21, 22)

20. Attend support group for spouses of homosexuals. (22)

21. Develop a plan regarding when, what, and how to tell children about spouse's homosexuality. (23)

22. Children will attend support group for children of homosexuals. (24)

—. _____
   _____
—. _____
   _____
—. _____
   _____

14. Assign homework for couple to list options available to them (e.g., divorcing, staying married with homosexual spouse honoring monogamy commitment, staying married and allowing for homosexual affairs).

15. Explore with clients their emotional reactions to each possible relationship continuation option and assist them in eliminating any that are unacceptable to their personal values.

16. Assist clients in identifying the emotional impact each option would have upon their children and assist them in identifying options that would best serve the needs of the children.

17. Encourage clients to make a conscious, mutual decision about which option to choose regarding their marriage.

18. Assist client(s) negotiating the terms and conditions relating to separation/divorce. Process disagreements in session with therapist.

19. Encourage client(s) to express the emotional reactions to loss of relationship.

20. Assist the client in identifying and understanding Campanaro-Cummings stages of grieving for heterosexuals married to homosexuals (Stage 1: Pre-Disclosure/Period of Discontent; Stage 2: Disclosure or ReDisclosure; Stage 3: Trial Accommodation and

Questioning; Stage 4: Aware-ness; Stage 5: Renegotiating the Relationship; Stage 6: Acceptance; Stage 7: Explora-tion and Detachment; Stage 8: Resolution).

21. Educate homosexual client about lesbian/gay resources in the community and encourage him/her to participate in them. (See Sexual Identity Confusion Adult chapter in this *Planner.*)

22. Refer client(s) to contact Inter-net sites, support groups and organizations for families of lesbians and gays (e.g., Family Pride Coalition, Parents & Friends of Lesbians and Gays, Children of Lesbians and Gays Everywhere).

23. Explore options with couple on ways to disclose and discuss parent's homosexuality with the children. (See Parenting Conflicts chapter in this *Planner.*)

24. Refer children to support group for children of lesbians/gays.

—. _____
    _____
—. _____
    _____
—. _____
    _____

DIAGNOSTIC SUGGESTIONS

Axis I:	296.xx	Major Depressive Disorder
	302.85	Gender Identity Disorder in Adolescents or Adults

309.0	Adjustment Disorder with Depressed Mood
309.24	Adjustment Disorder with Anxiety
309.28	Adjustment Disorder with Mixed Anxiety & Depressed Mood
309.4	Adjustment Disorder with Mixed Disturbance of Emotions and Conduct
300.4	Dysthymic Disorder
300.00	Anxiety Disorder NOS
300.02	Generalized Anxiety Disorder
311	Depressive Disorder NOS
313.82	Identity Problem
V61.1	Partner Relational Problem
V61.20	Parent-Child Relational Problem
_____	_____
_____	_____

HIV/AIDS

BEHAVIORAL DEFINITIONS

1. A positive test for human immunodeficiency virus (HIV).
2. Decreased immune functioning (e.g., decreased numbers of T-helper lymphocyte cells) secondary to HIV infection.
3. Physical symptoms such as chronic low-grade fever, persistent fatigue, diarrhea, unintentional weight loss, skin rash, and night sweats.
4. Diagnosis of acquired immune deficiency syndrome (AIDS).
5. Confusion, memory impairment, poor concentration.
6. Social withdrawal and lack of energy.
7. Feelings of hopelessness, worthlessness, or inappropriate guilt.
8. Diminished interest in or enjoyment of activities.
9. Not taking medications as prescribed.
10. Preoccupation with physical complaints grossly beyond what is expected for the state of HIV disease.
11. Refusing to acknowledge HIV positive status and need for medical care.
12. Engaging in unprotected sex.

—. _____
_____
—. _____
_____
—. _____
_____

LONG-TERM GOALS

1. Medically stabilize physical condition.
2. Increased knowledge about HIV/AIDS and medical treatment options.

3. Accept AIDS diagnosis/HIV status and pursue proper medical attention.
4. Alleviate depressed mood and return to previous level of functioning.
5. Differentiate between psychological and medical symptoms.
6. Stabilize anxiety level while increasing ability to function on a daily basis.
7. Clarify the degree of cognitive impairment.
8. Develop alternative coping strategies to compensate for cognitive limitations.
9. Eliminate high risk behaviors (e.g., intravenous drug use with unsterilized needles, unprotected sex) for transmitting HIV.
10. Improve communication with family, friends, and partners about disease and associated emotions.

—. _____
   _____
   _____
—. _____
   _____
   _____
—. _____
   _____

SHORT-TERM OBJECTIVES

1. Describe HIV/AIDS medical status openly and without denial. (1, 2, 3)

2. Decrease level of verbal denial regarding HIV status and/or AIDS diagnosis while increasing level of verbal acceptance. (3, 4)

3. Comply totally with doctor's orders for tests, medications, limitations, and/or treatments. (3, 4, 5, 6)

4. Increase knowledge of HIV and/or AIDS and its treatment. (6, 7, 23)

THERAPEUTIC INTERVENTIONS

1. Actively build the level of trust with the client in individual sessions through consistent eye contact, active listening, unconditional positive regard, and warm acceptance to help increase his/her ability to identify and express feelings.

2. Explore the client's understanding of his/her medical status.

3. Confront the denial of the HIV/AIDS status and of the necessity for follow through with medical protocol.

4. Monitor and document client's follow through on doctor's

5. Implement memory enhancing and coping strategies. (8)

6. Demonstrate responsibility by taking prescribed medications consistently and on time. (8, 9)

7. List the steps necessary for ongoing medical care for HIV or AIDS. (6, 9, 10)

8. Verbalize emotional, cognitive, and behavioral changes needed to improve health. (10, 11, 19, 23)

9. Identify emotional effects of being diagnosed with HIV/AIDS. (11, 15, 21, 23, 24)

10. Identify how emotions and behaviors have negatively impacted health. (11, 14)

11. Cooperate with and complete neuropsychological testing. (12, 13)

12. Begin to experience sadness in session while discussing the impact of AIDS on client's life. (14, 20, 21)

13. Identify negative self-talk that precipitates feelings of hopelessness and helplessness. (15, 16, 17)

14. Verbalize hopeful and positive statements regarding the future. (18, 23)

15. Implement behavioral strategies to reduce or eliminate irrational anxiety. (19, 22)

16. Verbalize an understanding of the secondary gain that results from physical complaints. (20, 21)

orders and redirect when client is failing to comply.

5. Make and necessary arrangements required for client to obtain the medical services needed.

6. Consult with physician and review doctor's orders with client.

7. Educate client about HIV/AIDS (e.g., means of transmission, chronic management, and available specialized services) through the use of didactics, videotape material, books, pamphlets, reliable Internet sites, and the like.

8. Assign and monitor memory enhancing activities/exercises (e.g., working a crossword puzzle, playing memory games) and memory loss coping strategies (e.g., writing lists, keep to a routine, utilizing medication-prompts).

9. Obtain medication schedule from doctor and enlist client's caregiver in monitoring compliance.

10. Process with client the necessary steps needed to ensure proper medical attention is obtained.

11. Help client identify and express his/her feelings connected with medical condition.

12. Refer and arrange for client to have neuropsychological testing to determine nature and degree of cognitive effects.

17. Identify the impact of HIV on social network. (21, 22, 23)

18. Increase the frequency of contact with others in social support system. (21, 22, 28)

19. Attend a support group for people with HIV/AIDS and their significant others. (23)

20. Verbalize any suicidal feelings, thoughts, or plans. (24)

21. Sign a no-harm contract. (25)

22. Verbalize awareness of and implement the practice of safer-sex techniques. (26, 28)

23. Identify and utilize appropriate health care, insurance, disability, and social service systems. (3, 10, 23, 27, 28)

24. Report on the increased frequency of assertive behaviors in various daily life situations. (17, 18, 22, 28)

25. Make a commitment to maintain a fighting spirit determined to overcome the physical, spiritual, and psychological threats of the medical crisis. (29)

26. Report instances of using laughter to reduce tension and anxiety. (29, 30)

27. Identify and implement positive dietary changes to maintain and support adequate level of nutrition and health. (31)

28. Utilize relaxation or meditation techniques to reduce stress. (32)

13. Administer appropriate psychological tests (e.g., WAIS-R) to assess cognitive functioning.

14. Encourage sharing feelings of depression in order to clarify them.

15. Assist in developing awareness of cognitive messages that reinforce hopelessness and helplessness.

16. Assign client to complete and process exercises on thought distortion related to helplessness in *Ten Days to Self-Esteem* (Burns).

17. Explore cognitive messages that mediate anxiety response.

18. Assist client in developing positive, realistic cognitive messages to replace those distortions that lead to helplessness, anxiety, and withdrawal.

19. Assist client in developing behavioral coping strategies (e.g., increased social involvement, obtaining employment, physical exercise) to counteract depression and anxiety.

20. Assist client in developing insight into the secondary gain received from physical illness, complaints, and the like.

21. Assess reactions of client's social network (e.g., friends, family, coworkers) and offer conjoint or family appointments to facilitate support for client.

22. Encourage and reinforce client's reaching out to others

29. Identify life priorities, goals, and aspirations, and develop a specific plan for implementing these. (33, 34)

___. _____
   _____
___. _____
   _____
___. _____
   _____

rather than isolating; process any emotional or cognitive obstacles (e.g., shame or distorted self-talk) to socialization.

23. Refer client to local AIDS service organization and encourage his/her active participation in available service (e.g., safer-sex education, support groups, case management, "buddy" program).

24. Assess and monitor suicidal behavior.

25. Have the client sign a no-harm contract that states he/she will do nothing to harm himself or herself while in treatment and will contact therapist if feeling suicidal.

26. Teach the details of safer sex practices and reinforce their consistent implementation.

27. Monitor client's use of social services available in the community and redirect when necessary.

28. Use modeling and behavior rehearsal to teach assertiveness in daily life situations (e.g., utilizing community resources, asking questions of medical personnel, reaching out socially, negotiating safer sex with partner).

29. Challenge the client to keep a positive, cheerful attitude, as free from anxiety as possible, to best create a biochemical, emotional, and spiritual atmosphere to fight disease and infirmity with healing powers.

Recommend reading *You Can Fight for Your Life* (LeShan) and/or *Anatomy of an Illness* (Cousins).

30. Instruct the client to find and read a book of humor or jokes and report on its effects on attitude and/or mood.

31. Refer client to nutritionist or dietician to help prevent undue weight loss and/or vitamin and mineral deficiencies.

32. Train client in the use of relaxation, visualization, and/or meditation techniques to manage stress and create a more peaceful frame of mind.

33. Assign client to make a list of "unfinished tasks" and life priorities. Assist client in developing a plan for completing important tasks and priorities.

34. Explore client's hopes and goals for the future and help client develop strategies for reaching these goals.

—. _____
   _____
—. _____
   _____
—. _____
   _____

DIAGNOSTIC SUGGESTIONS

Axis I:	296.2x	Major Depressive Disorder, Single Episode
	296.3x	Major Depression Disorder Recurrent
	300.02	Generalized Anxiety Disorder

316	[Specified Psychological Factor] Affecting . . . [Indicate the General Medical Condition]
316	Personality Traits or Coping Style Affecting . . . [Indicate the General Medical Condition]
316	Maladaptive Health Behaviors Affecting . . . [Indicate the General Medical Condition]
294.1	Dementia Due to . . . [Indicate the General Medical Condition]
309.0	Adjustment Disorder with Depressed Mood
300.4	Dysthymic Disorder
309.24	Adjustment Disorder with Anxiety
309.28	Adjustment Disorder with Mixed Anxiety and Depressed Mood
V15.81	Noncompliance with Treatment
_____	_____
_____	_____

HIV NEGATIVE/HIV POSITIVE COUPLE

BEHAVIORAL DEFINITIONS

1. Survivor's guilt experience by HIV negative partner.
2. HIV positive partner does not feel understood by HIV negative partner.
3. Sero-oppositive status have decreased couple's emotional bonds.
4. Fear of sexual contact by both partners.
5. Engaging in unsafe sexual practices.
6. Shame experienced by HIV negative partner.
7. HIV negative partner pretending to be HIV positive to "fit in" with peers.
8. Resentment by HIV negative partner of being forced into caregiving role.
9. Fear about losing HIV positive partner to death.
10. Fear of HIV negative partner leaving relationship.
11. Arguments about differing views about planning for the future.

—. _____
   _____
—. _____
   _____
—. _____
   _____

LONG-TERM GOALS

1. Acceptance of HIV negative sero-status and commitment to maintain HIV negative sero-status.
2. Resumption of healthy sexual contact by both partners.

3. Commitment to and practice of safer sexual contact.
4. Renewed commitment to relationship by both partners.
5. Acceptance of challenges unique to HIV positive/HIV negative (sero-oppositive couples) relationships.
6. Agreement and compromise about plans for the future and its impact on the relationship.
7. Decision to maintain or end the relationship.

—. _____
   _____
   _____

—. _____
   _____
   _____

—. _____
   _____

SHORT-TERM OBJECTIVES

1. Both partners attend and actively participate in conjoint sessions. (1)

2. Identify presenting problem in behavioral terms. (2)

3. Each partner identify feelings about the other's HIV sero-status (positive or negative). (3, 4, 5)

4. HIV negative partner accept and commit to maintaining uninfected status. (6, 7, 8)

5. Identify social structures to support HIV negative partner's identity as HIV negative and to assist him/her in maintaining sero-negative status. (7, 8)

6. Identify and interview sero-opposite couple role models. (9, 10)

7. Identify feelings (shame, secrecy, guilt, isolation,

THERAPEUTIC INTERVENTIONS

1. Schedule conjoint session and encourage attendance by both partners.

2. Assist client(s) in identifying presenting problem(s) in behavioral terms.

3. Explore the feelings associated with each client's sero-status.

4. Using role reversal technique, have each client describe feelings and behaviors believed to be experienced by his/her partner.

5. Support the couple in discussing the anxiety related to living with a life threatening illness.

6. Assist HIV negative partner in developing a healthy identity as an uninfected person.

7. Assist client(s) in identify social structures (e.g., safe-sex outreach groups, HIV Negative

alienation) associated with sero-negative status. (11)

8. HIV negative partner express and resolve dysfunctional feelings associated with sero-negative status. (12)

9. Identify factors that might lead to unsafe sexual practices. (13)

10. Describe current sexual practices and identify unsafe behaviors. (14)

11. Verbalize an understanding of safer sex practices. (15, 16)

12. Identify negative, dysfunctional thoughts that support unsafe sexual practices and replace with more realistic, positive thoughts to support safer sex practices. (17)

13. Attend HIV negative/HIV positive couple support group. (18)

14. Attend HIV negative support group. (19)

15. Demonstrate healthy communication skills. (20)

16. Spend less time talking about HIV/AIDS and increase socialization. (21, 22)

17. Verbalize an understanding of how internalized homophobia has affected the relationship. (23)

18. Identify pros and cons of remaining in the relationship. (24)

19. Develop a plan to cope with illness of HIV positive partner. (25, 26)

support groups) that support HIV negative partner's sero-status.

8. Encourage use of identified social structures to maintain HIV negative sero-status.

9. Have couple identify sero-opposite couple role models.

10. Have client(s) interview identified sero-opposite couple as to their experiences and coping techniques.

11. Assist HIV negative client in clarifying feelings (shame, secrecy, guilt, isolation, alienation) associated with sero-negative status.

12. Assist client in verbalizing these feelings to partner and resolving those that are dysfunctional.

13. Assist client(s) in identifying "triggers" (e.g., drug and/or alcohol use, unacceptable negative meanings associated with condom use) that lead to unsafe sexual practices.

14. Explore clients' current sexual behaviors and identify unsafe sexual practices.

15. Educate client(s) regarding safer sex techniques.

16. Refer clients to safer sex classes at community based HIV/AIDS organizations.

17. Explore the emotional reasons or beliefs for engaging in unsafe sexual practices and assist clients in replacing these

20. Discuss impact illness may have on the finances of the couple. (27, 28)

21. Identify and verbalize fears of abandonment and loneliness. (29, 30)

___. _____
_____
___. _____
_____
___. _____
_____

dysfunctional thoughts with more realistic thoughts that support safe sex practices.

18. Refer client(s) to HIV negative/ HIV positive support group.

19. Refer client to HIV negative support group.

20. Teach healthy communication skills (e.g., use of "I" messages, active listening) and encourage use by couple. (See Intimate Relationship Conflict chapter in this *Planner*.)

21. Assist client(s) in establishing "HIV-free zones" (i.e., place and/or time that couple agrees not to discuss HIV-related issues) to decrease emotional reactivity of living daily with HIV.

22. Assist client(s) in identifying socialization activities which are mutually satisfying and not HIV related; encourage their participation in them.

23. Explore client(s)' feelings of internalized homophobia and how it affects the relationship. (See Internalized Homophobia chapter in this *Planner*.)

24. Have client(s) list pros and cons of remaining in the relationship. Discuss key points with therapist.

25. Assist HIV negative partner in developing a plan to deal with illness of HIV positive partner.

26. Facilitate discussion of the wishes of HIV positive partner when faced with AIDS.

27. Facilitate a discussion about the impact illness may have on the finances of the couple.

28. Assist client(s) in identifying community resources available to help with the expenses of HIV positive individuals.

29. Facilitate client(s) talking about fears of abandonment and loneliness.

30. Facilitate the couple verbalizing the fear of abandonment to each other in session.

___. _____

_____

___. _____

_____

___. _____

_____

DIAGNOSTIC SUGGESTIONS

Axis I:	296.xx	Major Depressive Disorder
	300.4	Dysthymic Disorder
	293.83	Mood Disorder Due to . . . [Indicate the General Medical Condition]
	300.02	Generalized Anxiety Disorder
	309.0	Adjustment Disorder with Depressed Mood
	309.24	Adjustment Disorder with Anxiety
	309.28	Adjustment Disorder with Mixed Anxiety and Depressed Mood
	V61.9	Relational Problem Related to a Mental Disorder or General Medical Condition
	V61.1	Partner Relational Problem
	_____	_____
	_____	_____

INTERNALIZED HOMOPHOBIA

BEHAVIORAL DEFINITIONS

1. Discomfort with one's homosexuality.
2. Excessive fear and anxiety that sexual orientation will be discovered by others (e.g., family, friends, coworkers, strangers).
3. Avoidance of other gay/lesbian people.
4. Negative emotional reactions (e.g., anxiety, loathing, hatred) to gay men and lesbians who are open about their sexual orientation.
5. Prejudice and opposition to aspects of gay and lesbian relationships (e.g., parenting, commitment ceremonies, public displays of affection).
6. Rigid conformity to traditional gender roles (e.g., men must be competitive, strong, cool and tough; women must be passive, emotional, cooperative, and nurturing) that is causing significant conflict in interpersonal relationships.

—. _____
   _____
—. _____
   _____
—. _____
   _____

LONG-TERM GOALS

1. Acceptance of one's and other's homosexuality.
2. Perceiving other lesbian/gay men as sources of support, validation, and comfort.
3. Acceptance of all aspects of gay and lesbian relationships.
4. Establishment and maintenance of a satisfying lesbian/gay relationship.

—. _____
_____
—. _____
_____
—. _____
_____

SHORT-TERM OBJECTIVES

1. Verbalize thoughts, feelings, attitudes, and beliefs about homosexuality. (1, 2)

2. Identify negative attitudes and perceptions about lesbians/gay men. (2, 3, 4)

3. Verbalize an understanding of how homophobia was taught in childhood from family, peers, school, and so on. (2, 5)

4. Discuss fears and anxiety that sexual orientation will be discovered. (6)

5. List aspects of gay/lesbian relationships which cause discomfort. (7)

6. Identify automatic thoughts that contribute to homophobia (e.g., anxiety, fear). (8, 9)

7. Practice challenging distorted automatic thoughts and replacing them with more realistic, positive beliefs. (9)

8. Both partners describe conflict over disclosing nature of relationship to significant others. (10)

THERAPEUTIC INTERVENTIONS

1. Probe client about thoughts, feelings, attitude, and beliefs about homosexuality.

2. Conduct a comprehensive bi-opsychosocial assessment including questions about level of interaction with gay men/lesbians, to whom client has disclosed sexual identity, and age at which sexual orientation was "discovered."

3. Assist client in identifying negative attitudes and perceptions about lesbians/gay men.

4. Using a solution-focused approach, ask client "If there were a pill that you could take that would make you heterosexual would you take it?" Follow up with questions about how client's life would be different to identify perceptions distorted by homophobic beliefs/perceptions.

5. Explore client's childhood experiences with homophobia in school, family, church, and so on.

9. Identify social relationships in which sexual identity is kept secret. (11)

10. List pros and cons of socializing with other gay men and lesbians. (11, 12)

11. Discuss fears of appearing too masculine or feminine. (13)

12. Identify current attitudes, beliefs and feelings about sex roles. (14, 15)

13. Verbalize an understanding of how rigid conformity to traditional sex roles has negatively impacted emotional, psychological and social health. (16)

14. Read books on homophobia. (17)

15. Verbalize an increased knowledge of homophobia. (17, 18)

16. Participate in social activities with other lesbians and gay men. (19)

17. Identify homosexual role models that serve to increase level of pride in gay/lesbian identity and decrease level of shame, embarrassment, and so on. (20)

___. _____
_____

___. _____
_____

___. _____
_____

6. Explore fears and anxiety that sexual orientation will be discovered. (See chapter on Sexual Identity Confusion–Adult in this *Planner.*)

7. Ask client to list aspects of gay/lesbian relationship (e.g., parenting, commitment ceremonies) which cause discomfort.

8. Educate client about the use of an automatic thought record and assign him/her to use throughout the week to identify homophobic beliefs (e.g., I can never have a relationship because I'm lesbian/gay, I don't like any gay men/lesbians because they are too feminine/masculine, all lesbians/gay men are the same).

9. Confront client's homophobic statements, beliefs, and so on, and assist him/her in replacing with more realistic, positive beliefs.

10. Probe clients about conflict in relationship. (See chapter on Intimate Partner Conflict in this *Planner.*)

11. Have client draw an Eco-Map depicting social relationships (e.g., church, family of origin, social network) with homosexuals and heterosexuals to determine current level of social interaction within the gay/lesbian community and all areas where client is hiding sexual identity.

12. Have client list pros and cons of socializing with other lesbians and gay men.

13. Explore feelings (e.g., shame, fear, anxiety) about appearing too masculine/feminine.

14. Administer standardized tests (e.g., Bem Sex Role Inventory, MMPI) that measure client's gender role attitudes.

15. Inquire about client's perceptions of gender roles by asking questions about what he/she believes women's and men's roles should be in a variety of personal and social situations.

16. Confront client with consequences of rigidly adhering to traditional sex roles (e.g., man afraid to be gentle with partner because of fear of appearing too feminine, woman afraid to be assertive sexually for fear of being too masculine).

17. Assign client to read books about homophobia (e.g., *Overcoming Heterosexism and Homophobia* [Sears & Williams] or *Homophobia: We All Pay The Price* [Blumenfeld]).

18. Educate client about homophobia.

19. Educate client about social activities for lesbians/gay men (e.g., food clubs, political groups, bookstore readings, bowling clubs) and encourage him/her to attend one that matches interests.

20. Assign client homework of identifying individuals whom he/she respects that are homosexual through the use of public library, Internet, and bookstores.

—. _____
   _____
—. _____
   _____
—. _____
   _____

DIAGNOSTIC SUGGESTIONS

Axis I: 300.4   Dysthymic Disorder
              302.85   Gender Identity Disorder in Adolescents or Adults
              309.0   Adjustment Disorder with Depressed Mood
              309.24   Adjustment Disorder with Anxiety
              309.28   Adjustment Disorder with Mixed Anxiety and Depressed Mood
              V61.1   Partner Relational Problem
              _____   _____
              _____   _____

Axis II: 301.81   Narcissistic Personality Disorder
              _____   _____
              _____   _____

INTIMATE RELATIONSHIP CONFLICTS

BEHAVIORAL DEFINITIONS

1. Frequent or continual arguing with significant other.
2. Lack of communication with significant other.
3. Infidelity committed by one or both partners.
4. A pattern of angry projection of responsibility for the conflicts onto the other party.
5. Pending separation.
6. A pattern of spending all time together without involvement in individual interests and activities and without socializing with other couples or individuals.
7. A pattern of disagreement about household responsibilities, financial arrangements, sexual roles, and decision making.

—. _____
   _____
—. _____
   _____
   _____
—. _____
   _____

LONG-TERM GOALS

1. Decrease amount of time spent arguing and increase amount of enjoyable time spent together.
2. Develop new interpersonal skills which assist couple in resolving conflicts and improving overall satisfaction with relationship.
3. Accept the termination of the relationship.
4. Make a commitment to one intimate relationship at a time.

5. Acceptance of partner forgiveness for infidelities.
6. Decision to end relationship.
7. Develop a balance of individual and couple activities that support the relationship.
8. Choose mutually agreed upon roles in the relationship.

—. _____
    _____
—. _____
    _____
—. _____
    _____

SHORT-TERM OBJECTIVES

1. Arrange, attend, and actively participate in conjoint sessions with significant other. (1)

2. Identify current roles (sexual, financial management, house-keeping, etc.), how they were assumed, and how they contribute to the relationship conflict. (2)

3. List the positive aspects of the present relationship. (3)

4. Verbalize an understanding of the different causes of the relationship conflict(s). (5)

5. Identify family of origin relationship patterns and how it impacts current relationship. (5, 6)

6. Identify any physical, sexual, or verbal abuse in relationship and commit to eliminating it. (7)

7. Identify a pattern of continually forming harmful and/or

THERAPEUTIC INTERVENTIONS

1. Facilitate conjoint sessions with significant other with focus on increasing communication and learning problem solving skills.

2. Assign couple to write an autobiography of the relationship starting with the first date and including milestones (initial sexual encounter, sharing residence, buying a house, etc.), roles assumed by each partner, fidelity agreement, major conflicts and how decisions have been made in the relationship. Process with therapist.

3. Assign client homework of listing positive interactions between them throughout the week as well as positive traits of partner. Process in session.

4. Explore the nature of current, ongoing conflicts regarding the relationship.

dissatisfactory intimate relationships. (8)

8. Verbalize an understanding of the connection between substance abuse and the conflicts present within the relationship. (9)

9. Partner abusing drugs and alcohol agrees to abstain from same or seek treatment for chemical dependence.

10. Identify or rule out sexual dysfunction. (11, 12)

11. Each partner list the changes he/she would like from the other to improve the relationship. (13)

12. Each client agrees to and implements behavioral changes requested by partner. (14, 15)

13. Verbalize expectations for the relationship. (16)

14. Demonstrate new conflict resolution techniques in session. (17, 18, 19, 20)

15. Read books on relationship building and commitment within gay and lesbian relationships. (19, 21)

16. Both partners agree to set aside time each week to discuss conflict. (20)

17. Acknowledge any and all instances of infidelity. (22)

18. Identify the impact of infidelity on relationship. (23)

19. Discuss emotional barriers to intimacy and committing to a monogamous relationship. (24)

5. Explore family relationship history with clients and assist them in developing an understanding of how these have impacted current relationship.

6. Assign each client to complete a genogram and then share in conjoint session his/her genogram with the other to promote greater empathy and awareness concerning each other.

7. Assess for physical, sexual, and/or verbal abuse and refer partners to specialized treatment services. (See Physical Abuse Victim chapter in this *Planner.*)

8. Gather personal history of each partner as to previous dysfunctional intimate relationships.

9. Explore the role of substance abuse in precipitating conflict and/or abuse in the relationship.

10. Solicit agreement for substance abuse treatment for the chemically dependent partner. (See Chemical Dependence chapter in this *Planner.*)

11. Explore with couple the nature of their sexual relationship to determine or rule out any sexual issues. (See Female Sexual Dysfunction and Male Sexual Dysfunction chapter in this *Planner.*)

12. Make referral to a physician who specializes in treating the medical aspects of sexual dysfunction for an evaluation.

20. Unfaithful partner participate in treatment for sexually compulsive behavior and/or addiction. (25)

21. Unfaithful partner accept responsibility for infidelity. (26)

22. Unfaithful partner verbalize plan to make amends to hurt partner. (27)

23. Hurt partner accept apology for partner's infidelity and state willingness to begin forgiveness process. (28)

24. List pros and cons of remaining in the relationship. (29)

25. Hurt partner identify cognitive distortions related to infidelity and replace with more realistic beliefs. (30)

26. Discuss the level of closeness/distance desired in a relationship and how this may relate to fears of intimacy. (31)

27. Verbalize an understanding of the process of merging and the need for each partner to maintain separate identities. (32, 33)

28. Increase time spent in individual activities. (34, 35, 36)

29. Increase time spent in enjoyable contact with partner. (36, 37)

30. Engage in social activities that are supportive of gay and lesbian relationships. (37)

31. Identify and verbalize issues of internalized homophobia in the relationship and how they contribute to the conflicts. (38, 39)

13. Assign each partner a list of changes the other needs to make to improve the relationship.

14. Seek a commitment from each partner to commit to requested behavioral changes.

15. In conjoint sessions, process changes each partner believes are necessary to improve the relationship.

16. Confront irrational beliefs and unrealistic expectations regarding the relationship and then assist couple in adopting more realistic beliefs and expectations of each other and the relationship.

17. Assist each partner in clarifying communication and expression of feelings within sessions.

18. Train in assertiveness skills (e.g., broken record technique, negative inquiry).

19. Teach the couple intimacy exercises (e.g., for men assign the exercises from *Intimacy Between Men* [Driggs & Finn] and for women assign the exercises from *Lesbian Sex* [Loulan]) such as "fighting fair" and "anger communication" and have them practice these techniques in session and at home.

20. Assign client homework of limiting discussion of conflict to scheduled time each week.

21. Assign clients to read book(s) focusing on gay/lesbian

32. Decide whether or not to end the relationship. (40)

—. _____
   _____
—. _____
   _____
—. _____
   _____

relationships (e.g., *The Intimacy Dance* [Berzon], *The Lesbian & Gay Book of Love & Marriage* [Martinac], *Lesbian Couples* [Clunis & Green], *Love Between Men* [Isensee], *Permanent Partners* [Berzon], *Intimacy Between Men* [Driggs & Finn]). Process key ideas with therapist.

22. Explore for a history of infidelity within the relationship.

23. Assess the impact of infidelity on the relationship.

24. Probe client about emotional barriers (e.g., fear of rejection, lack of trust, low self-esteem) to intimacy and commitment to a monogamous relationship.

25. Refer client to treatment (e.g., individual psychotherapy, group therapy, residential treatment) for sexually compulsive behavior and/or sexual addiction. (See Sexual Acting Out chapter in this *Planner*.)

26. Encourage client to accept responsibility for infidelity and positively reinforce any movement toward that goal.

27. Assist client in developing a plan for amends (e.g., recommitment to relationship, continue couple's counseling).

28. Have hurt partner verbalize acceptance of apology and willingness to begin the forgiveness process.

29. Have client(s) list pros and cons of remaining in relationship.

30. Assist client in identifying cognitive distortions related to the infidelity (e.g., I can never trust him/her again, I'll never feel like having sex again) and train client how to replace with more realistic beliefs (e.g., It will take time to trust him/her again. Eventually I'll probably feel like having sex again).

31. Explore each partner's fears regarding getting too close and feeling vulnerable to hurt, rejection, or abandonment.

32. Educate couple about the process of merging individual identities into that of a couple and the need for each partner to maintain a separate identity.

33. Assign couple to read *Lesbian Psychologies* (Boston Lesbian Psychologies Collective) or *Lesbian Couples* (Clunis & Green); process key points with therapist.

34. Assist each client in identifying individual activities that he/she would find pleasurable and encourage participation in these activities.

35. Probe the issue of fear of spending time away from partner.

36. Assign client's to complete schedule that details social activities for one week and how they positively and negatively affected the relationship.

37. Refer clients to lesbian/gay oriented social activities (e.g., gay bowling clubs, hiking clubs,

food clubs) and encourage participation.

38. Probe each partner about negative beliefs regarding homosexual relationships (e.g., gay men are promiscuous, gay/lesbian relationships do not last, lesbian "bed death" in inevitable) and educate about the facts.

39. Assist clients in identifying issues of internalized homophobia and how they contribute to the conflict. (See Internalized Homophobia chapter in this *Planner*.)

40. Encourage client to set a date by which he/she will decide whether or not to end the relationship. (See Separation chapter of this *Planner*.)

—. _____
_____
—. _____
_____
—. _____
_____

DIAGNOSTIC SUGGESTIONS

Axis I: 296.xx   Major Depressive Disorder
309.0   Adjustment Disorder with Depressed Mood
309.24   Adjustment Disorder with Anxiety
309.28   Adjustment Disorder with Mixed Anxiety and Depressed Mood
302.71   Hypoactive Sexual Desire Disorder
V61.1   Partner Relational Problem
_____   _____
_____   _____

Axis II: 301.50   Histrionic Personality Disorder
                 301.6   Dependent Personality Disorder
                 301.81   Narcissistic Personality Disorder
                 301.82   Avoidant Personality Disorder
                 301.9   Personality Disorder NOS

_____   _____

_____   _____

LEGAL CONFLICTS

BEHAVIORAL DEFINITIONS

1. Arrests and legal charges related to sexual behavior.
2. Legal issues (discrimination, estate planning, etc.) related to HIV/AIDS.
3. Discrimination and harassment experienced on the job.
4. History of trouble with the law due to substance abuse/dependence.
5. Discharge from the military due to sexual orientation.
6. Estate planning.
7. Difficulties with immigration due to sexual orientation and/or HIV/AIDS.

—. _____
  _____
—. _____
  _____
—. _____
  _____

LONG-TERM GOALS

1. Accept responsibility for acts related to arrest(s) due to sexual behavior.
2. Resolve legal issues related to HIV/AIDS.
3. Develop an understanding of workplace discrimination and take steps to minimize effects on physical and emotional well-being.
4. Accept responsibility for violations of the law due to substance use and seek treatment for such.
5. Resolve emotional consequences related to discharge from prison.
6. Complete estate planning.
7. Resolve immigration issues.

___. _____

___. _____

___. _____

SHORT-TERM OBJECTIVES

1. Honestly disclose the facts leading to arrest. (1)

2. Verbalize emotions related to arrest/legal conflict. (2)

3. Verbalize an acceptance of responsibility for actions that led to illegal activity and arrest. (3)

4. Identify reasons for engaging in illegal sexual behavior. (4, 5)

5. Attend sexual compulsives support group. (6)

6. List legal issues related to HIV/AIDS (e.g., estate planning, durable power of attorney for health care). (7, 8)

7. Discuss wishes regarding life-sustaining treatment while partner is in session. (9)

8. Designate a durable power of attorney for health care and complete all forms. (10)

9. Identify substance abuse related to behaviors that have led to legal problems. (11, 12)

10. Attend 12-Step support group and seek treatment for chemical dependence. (13, 14)

THERAPEUTIC INTERVENTIONS

1. Inquire as to behaviors that led to arrest and assess the role that psychopathology (e.g., chemical dependence, sexual acting out) plays in current conflict.

2. Explore the emotional reactions to arrest/legal conflict and provide validation through active listening.

3. Confront client with history of pattern of illegal behavior (e.g., driving while intoxicated, sex in public places) and encourage him/her to accept responsibility for behavior that led to arrest.

4. Review behaviors that led to arrest while focusing upon any emotional triggers that contributed to behavior.

5. Assist client in identifying reasons for engaging in illegal sexual behavior. (See Sexual Acting Out chapter in this *Planner.*)

6. Refer client to a sexual compulsive support group.

7. Educate client about legal issues related to HIV/AIDS.

11. Develop plan to reestablish life as a civilian (e.g., obtain housing, employment) after release from prison. (15)

12. Verbalize an understanding of the legal issues regarding living as a lesbian/gay couple (e.g., buying a house, estate planning, custody of children). (16, 17, 18, 19)

13. Verbalize an increased knowledge of legal issues specific to lesbians/gay men. (17, 18)

14. Read books about legal issues regarding lesbians/gay men. (18)

15. Consult with an attorney. (19)

16. Identify community resources that may assist with resolving legal conflict. (20)

17. Finalize decisions regarding estate planning (e.g., beneficiaries of estate, division of property). (21)

18. Discuss custody of children in the event of chronic illness or death. (21, 22)

19. Develop custody plan for children in the event of chronic illness or death. (23, 24, 25)

___. _____

_____

___. _____

_____

___. _____

_____

8. Ask client to list legal issues related to HIV/AIDS.

9. Arrange conjoint session with partner and facilitate discussion of health care decisions.

10. Assist client with designating durable power of attorney for health care and completing necessary paper work.

11. Review consequences of substance abuse with client. Confront any minimization.

12. Conduct an assessment of client's substance abuse including which substances have been abused, how frequently they are used, and consequences of abuse (e.g., arrests, relationship conflicts).

13. Refer client to 12-Step support group (e.g., AA, NA,). Encourage and monitor attendance.

14. Refer or provide treatment for chemical dependence. (See Chemical Dependence chapter in this *Planner*.)

15. Assist client in developing a plan to reestablish life as a civilian after release from prison.

16. Educate client regarding the legal issues (e.g., estate planning, child custody) related to living as a lesbian/gay couple.

17. Educate client regarding the legal issues (e.g., employment discrimination, durable power of attorney for health care, estate planning) specific to gay men and lesbians.

18. Assign client to read books that provide information about gay/lesbian related legal issues (e.g., *A Legal Guide for Lesbian and Gay Couples* [Curry, Clifford, & Leonard]).

19. Refer client to an attorney specializing in the area of legal conflict related to gays and lesbians (e.g., immigration, workplace discrimination, child custody, estate planning, entrapment).

20. Educate client about the community resources available to assist in resolving legal conflict (e.g., Lambda Legal Defense & Education Fund, ACLU, GLAAD).

21. Encourage client(s) to finalize estate planning. Process any resistance.

22. Assist client in disclosing estate planning decisions to significant others (e.g., partner, friends, family) by including them in session and facilitating discussion.

23. Assist client in identifying which individual(s) he/she wants to assign custody of the children in event of chronic illness or death.

24. Educate client about the laws regarding child custody in her/his state. Assist him/her in identifying undesired consequences of not legally specifying to whom custody should be designated (e.g., child's custody would revert to state,

grandparents would be granted
custody instead of life partner).

25. Assist client in developing a
chid custody plan and encourage its legal completion.

—. _____
   _____
—. _____
   _____
—. _____
   _____

DIAGNOSTIC SUGGESTIONS

Axis I:	304.80	Polysubstance Dependence
	305.00	Alcohol Abuse
	305.70	Amphetamine Abuse
	305.20	Cannabis Abuse
	305.60	Cocaine Abuse
	309.0	Adjustment Disorder with Depressed Mood
	309.24	Adjustment Disorder with Anxiety
	309.28	Adjustment Disorder with Mixed Anxiety and Depressed Mood
	309.4	Adjustment Disorder with Mixed Disturbance of Emotions and Conduct
	_____	_____
	_____	_____
Axis II:	301.7	Antisocial Personality Disorder
	301.81	Narcissistic Personality Disorder
	_____	_____
	_____	_____

MALE SEXUAL DYSFUNCTION

BEHAVIORAL DEFINITIONS

1. Recurrent lack of the ability to attain or maintain an erection.
2. Inability to achieve orgasm during pleasurable sexual activity.
3. Recurrent premature ejaculation.
4. Consistent aversion and/or avoidance of all sexual contact in spite of a caring interpersonal relationship.
5. Avoidance of sex due to fears of contacting HIV or other sexually transmitted diseases (STDs).
6. Decrease in sexual desire due to medical disorder (e.g., HIV/AIDS).
7. Sense of discomfort with sexual role (e.g., being anally penetrated, assuming passive role).
8. Expression of shame or rejection of one's own body that consistently leads to decrease or lack of sexual activity.

—. _____
   _____
   _____
—. _____
   _____
   _____
—. _____
   _____

LONG-TERM GOALS

1. Increase the frequency, range of, and satisfaction with sexual activity within the couple.
2. Increase desire and sense of enjoyment in sexual activities.
3. Achieve ability to attain and maintain an erection.
4. Ability to achieve an orgasm during pleasurable sexual activity.
5. Increase knowledge of HIV/AIDS and other sexually transmitted diseases (STDs) and modes of transmission.

6. Accept medical diagnosis and its impact on sexual life.
7. Reduce homophobic beliefs, anxiety, fear, and shame about sexuality that have inhibited sexual pleasure.
8. Reach level of acceptance about body image.
9. Engage in a range of mutually agreed upon sexual activities which are a source of pleasure.

——. _____
   _____
   _____
——. _____
   _____
   _____
——. _____
   _____

SHORT-TERM OBJECTIVES

1. Verbalize an increased knowledge of HIV/AIDS and other sexually transmitted diseases (STDs), their modes of transmission, and impact on sexual life. (1, 2)

2. Identify emotional effects of being diagnosed with HIV/AIDS. (1, 2, 3)

3. Identify impact of HIV/AIDS on sexual activity. (2, 4)

4. Commit to attend and participate in conjoint sessions with partner. (5)

5. Verbalize the nature and history of the sexual problem and how it has impacted values, beliefs, and actions in the nonsexual aspects of the relationship. (6, 7)

6. Identify sexual problem and treatment goals in behavioral terms. (6, 8)

THERAPEUTIC INTERVENTIONS

1. Educate client about HIV/AIDS and other sexually transmitted diseases (STDs) though the use of didactics, videotape material, books, pamphlets, reliable Internet sites and the like.

2. Teach the details of safer sex practices and reinforce consistent implementation.

3. Assist the client in identifying emotional effects of being diagnosed with HIV/AIDS. (See HIV/AIDS chapter in this _Planner._)

4. Explore the impact the diagnosis of HIV/AIDS has had on sexual relations.

5. Educate client(s) about the need for both partners to participate in sexual counseling and press for commitment for both members to attend and participate.

7. Describe and clarify sexual roles and practices of each partner. (8, 13)

8. Verbalize beliefs associated with assuming passive sexual role (e.g., being anally penetrated is more like a woman, to be a man you have to be aggressive). (8, 11)

9. Verbalize an understanding of the impact of nonsexual relationship conflicts upon satisfaction with sexual activities. (9, 10)

10. Identify any stressors outside the relationship which may be affecting sexual satisfaction. (12)

11. Describe sexual history of each partner and the couple. (13, 14)

12. Describe childhood experiences that have contributed to feelings of anxiety, fear, and shame about sexuality. (15, 16, 22)

13. Verbalize an understanding of how religious training has negatively impacted sexual functioning. (16, 17)

14. Identify any sexual abuse history. (18)

15. Verbalize an understanding of the impact of childhood sexual abuse upon current sexual problems and resolve emotional barriers to satisfaction. (19, 20)

16. Verbalize the situations and behaviors needed for each

6. Assist the client(s) in describing sexual problem and treatment goals in behavioral terms (e.g., both partners dissatisfied with sex once a month and want to increase it to once a week, partner would like to be able to achieve orgasm during couple's sexual activities).

7. Assign client(s) homework that asks each partner to write a description of their relationship after the sexual problem is resolved. Have partners read description to each other in session.

8. Inquire as to each partner's current sexual roles and activities (e.g., who initiates sex, which activities are performed by whom) and explore the degree of satisfaction with current practices.

9. Probe about conflicts and disagreements outside of the arena of sexual relations.

10. Assist client(s) in understanding connection between relationship conflicts and sexual dissatisfaction.

11. Explore beliefs associated with assuming the passive role and assist client in replacing beliefs with healthy alternatives.

12. Explore areas of stress (e.g., work, social relationships, financial problems) that may be contributing to sexual difficulties.

13. Inquire about the sexual history of couple including previous

partner to feel safe during sexual activity. (21)

17. Verbalize an understanding of the role of family of origin experiences in the development of negative sexual attitudes and responses. (16, 22)

18. Verbalize an understanding of how internalized homophobia contributes to fear, shame, and anxiety during sex and resolve homophobic beliefs. (23, 30)

19. Identify automatic thoughts that increase anxiety, fear, and shame during sexual activities. (24)

20. Replace negative dysfunctional cognitions with positive, reality-based thoughts that promote sexual acceptance and pleasure. (25)

21. Verbalize an understanding of how male sexual objectification has contributed to negative body image and inhibited sexual pleasure. (26, 30)

22. Complete a list of all anxiety/guilt provoking sexual activities. (27, 31)

23. Practice deep muscle relaxation techniques. (28)

24. Practice *in vivo* desensitization exercises using deep muscle relaxation and hierarchy of activities that provoke anxiety/guilt. (29)

25. Read and discuss books assigned on men's/gay men's sexuality. (30)

activities enjoyed, frequency, and how activities were negotiated within the couple.

14. Ask each partner to describe his sexual history prior to this relationship focusing upon information, attitudes, and emotions about sexuality in general and homosexuality specifically.

15. Ask each partner to describe where, what, and when they learned about sexuality in general and homosexuality in particular.

16. Explore role of family of origin in teaching negative attitudes regarding sexuality, homosexuality, and men.

17. Explore role of religious training in reinforcing feelings of guilt and shame surrounding homosexuality, sexual behavior, and thoughts. (See Religious Conflicts chapter in this *Planner.*)

18. Explore client's history for experience of sexual trauma or abuse.

19. Educate client(s) about the impact of childhood sexual abuse upon sexual problems.

20. Process emotions surrounding an emotional trauma in the sexual arena. (See Sexual Abuse Chapter in this *Planner.*)

21. Using a solution-focused approach, ask each partner to identify what they need to feel safe before, during, and after sexual activity.

26. Speak freely and accurately regarding sexuality issues. (31)

27. Abstain from substance abuse patterns that interfere with sexual response. (32)

28. Verbalize an understanding of the role physical disease or medication has on sexual dysfunction. (33)

29. Cooperate with a physician's complete examination and report results. (34)

30. Describe any signs and symptoms of depression. (35, 36)

31. Verbalize an understanding of the impact of depression upon sexual problem(s). (35)

32. Identify and participate in a strategy to alleviate depression. (36)

33. Acknowledge any infidelity that has occured, discussing feelings surrounding the infidelity and making a commitment to fidelity agreement. (37)

34. Practice saying no to sexual activities which are not desired and/or anxiety provoking. (38)

35. Identify and experiment with sexual aids that may increase pleasure. (39)

36. Report an increase in ability to maintain an erection. (40)

37. Report a decrease in premature ejaculation. (41, 42)

38. Practice sensate focus exercise. (43, 44, 45)

22. Explore sex role models client(s) experienced in childhood or adolescence.

23. Probe client(s) for homophobic beliefs and educate about the impact upon sexual pleasure. Assist client(s) in developing positive beliefs. (See Internalized Homophobia chapter in this *Planner.*)

24. Educate client(s) about the nature of automatic thoughts and ask them to describe what comes to mind before, during and after sexual activity.

25. Assist client(s) in challenging negative automatic thoughts.

26. Educate client(s) about the negative effects of sexual objectification on body image and sexual pleasure.

27. Assign a hierarchy listing activities (e.g., being nude with partner, having oral sex) that provoke anxiety/guilt on a scale of 1 to 10.

28. Teach client(s) deep muscle relaxation techniques.

29. Assign client(s) graduated *in vivo* desensitization exercises using hierarchy of activities that provoke anxiety/guilt and deep relaxation techniques. Have client(s) start with the least anxiety/guilt provoking activities and move up the hierarchy as negative emotions decrease to tolerable levels.

30. Assign books (e.g., *Gay Sex: A Manual for Men Who Love*

39. Write a journal of sexual fantasies, beliefs, and attitudes that stimulate sexual arousal. (46, 47)

40. Communicate sexual desires to partner. (47, 48)

41. List sexual activities which couple has mutually agreed to explore. (30, 48)

42. Experiment with new mutually agreed upon sexual activities and settings. (48, 49)

43. Identify sexual activities that are mutually satisfying and stimulating. (50)

44. Verbalize agreement as to whether or not to include anal penetration in sexual activities. (48, 50)

45. Report increase in overall sexual activity, satisfaction, and pleasure within the couple. (51)

——. _____
   _____

——. _____
   _____

——. _____
   _____

Men [Hart], _Sex Advisor: The 100 Most Asked Questions About Sex Between Men_ [Palermo], _Love Between Men_ [Isensee]) that provide accurate sexual information.

31. Reinforce client(s) talking freely, knowledgeably, and positively regarding sexual thoughts, feelings, and behavior.

32. Educate client(s) about impact of substance abuse upon sexuality and press for agreement for abstinence.

33. Review medications taken by client(s) with regard to their possible negative side effects on sexual functioning.

34. Refer to a gay male sensitive physician for a complete physical to rule out any organic basis for dysfunction.

35. Assess for depression and educate client(s) about the impact of depression.

36. Assist client(s) in developing strategies to deal with depression including individual psychotherapy and/or referral to a medical professional for prescription of antidepressants. (See Depression chapter in this _Planner_.)

37. Review any sexual relationships outside the couple's fidelity contract and discuss its impact upon the couple's sexual relationship. (See Intimate Relationship Conflicts chapter in this _Planner_.)

38. Encourage client(s) to assertively refuse any sexual activities which are not desired and/or anxiety provoking.

39. Educate client(s) about use of sexual aids (e.g., gay male erotica, dildos, lotions) that may increase sexual pleasure.

40. Refer to physician for medical interventions for impotence (e.g., Viagra, pump).

41. Educate client(s) about squeeze technique for premature ejaculation.

42. Have client practice squeeze technique and report about progress with therapist in session.

43. Assign sensate focus homework (e.g., ask couple to provide one another gentle touch and massage avoiding genital stimulation).

44. Assign clients to alternate stimulating each other's genitals but proscribe orgasm. Encourage partner who is being stimulated to direct the speed and intensity of the stimulation.

45. Explore reactions to sensate focus exercises and assist client(s) in identifying any sources of conflict.

46. Assign client(s) to keep a journal of sexual fantasies, feelings, and thoughts.

47. Ask client(s) to describe sexual fantasies, feelings, and thoughts from journal and

discuss which are mutually stimulating and interesting.

48. Ask client(s) to decide which sexual activities they would like to explore. Process any disagreement.

49. Assign couple to begin experimenting with new sexual activities. Process reactions, success, and failure with therapist in session.

50. Ask couple to identify which activities are a source of pleasure and encourage them to continue to participate in them.

51. Inquire as to how often the couple is engaging in sexual activity and reinforce progress.

___. _____

_____

___. _____

_____

___. _____

_____

DIAGNOSTIC SUGGESTIONS

Axis I:	302.71	Hypoactive Sexual Desire Disorder
	302.79	Sexual Aversion Disorder
	302.72	Male Erectile Disorder
	302.74	Male Orgasmic Disorder
	302.76	Dyspareunia [Not Due to a General Medical Condition]
	302.75	Premature Ejaculation
	608.89	Male Hypoactive Sexual Disorder Due to . . . [Indicate the General Medical Condition]
	607.84	Male Erectile Disorder Due to . . . [Indicate the General Medical Condition]
	608.89	Male Dyspareunia Due to . . . [Indicate the General Medical Condition]

302.70	Sexual Dysfunction NOS
995.5	Sexual Abuse of Child if Focus of Clinical Attention is on the Victim
V61.1	Partner Relational Problem
296.xx	Major Depressive Disorder
300.4	Dysthymic Disorder
300.7	Body Dysmorphic Disorder
——	————————————————
——	————————————————

PARENTING CONFLICTS

BEHAVIORAL DEFINITIONS

1. Disagreement between partners about parenting roles and methods.
2. No social relationships (e.g., friendships with other parents, membership in PTA) that support the parental role.
3. Conflict with, and/or a lack of support from, "in-laws" about raising a child.
4. Child is uncomfortable with parent's sexual orientation.
5. Child is unwilling to introduce peers to parents or include peers in family activities.
6. Child has questions about family's structure and/or parent's sexuality.
7. Child is experiencing academic problems (e.g., falling grades, truancy suspension).
8. Child is subjected to homophobia (e.g., teasing, physical violence from others) in school and/or other social settings.
9. Conflict between family members resulting from the blending of families.
10. Impending custody or legal issues involving the children in a gay/lesbian family.
11. One parent has a life-threatening illness (e.g., AIDS, Breast Cancer).

___. _____
_____
___. _____
_____
___. _____
_____

LONG-TERM GOALS

1. Agreement about parenting roles and methods.
2. Develop and demonstrate appropriate parenting skills.
3. Understand emotional, legal, and financial commitments necessary to raise a child to adulthood.
4. Engage in a variety of social relationships that are supportive of parenting role.
5. Development of strategies to cope with prejudices that confront parent(s) and child in gay/lesbian families.
6. Child has increased comfort with gay/lesbian parents.
7. Child demonstrates increased willingness to include peers in family's activities.
8. Decreased emotional discomfort by child being subjected to homophobia in school and/or social settings.
9. Child returns to previous level of academic functioning.
10. A cessation of yelling, fighting, and arguing among family members.
11. Understand the custody of legal issues that may confront gay/lesbian families.
12. Understand the impact a life-threatening illness will have on the family.

—. _____
  _____
—. _____
  _____
—. _____
  _____

SHORT-TERM OBJECTIVES	THERAPEUTIC INTERVENTIONS
1. Openly discuss emotions about conflict and/or problems in family. (1)	1. Actively build level of trust with the client(s) to help them identify and express feelings and beliefs.
2. Attend and actively participate in family therapy sessions. (2)	2. Explain the importance of dealing with problems with entire family and press for commitment from all family
3. Cooperate with comprehensive biopsychosocial assessment of family. (3)	

4. Identify any abuse of the child. (3, 4)

5. Identify child rearing problem(s) in behavioral terms (e.g., parents arguing about discipline methods, child is failing in school). (5, 10)

6. Identify any experiences of harassment and/or violence child is experiencing because of having gay/lesbian parents. (6, 7)

7. Take all steps necessary to ensure safety of child. (3, 8)

8. Child attends peer support group. (9)

9. Verbalize disagreements couple has about parenting roles, discipline methods, and/or caretaking responsibilities. (10)

10. Identify any financial stressors that are contributing to conflicts in the family. (11)

11. Verbalize an understanding of how custody and legal conflicts are negatively impacting the family. (12, 13)

12. Verbalize an understanding the impact a life-threatening illness has, and will have, on the family (e.g., change in parenting roles, future custody issues, parent becoming sick). (13, 14, 15)

13. Make a plan for the future care of child in the case of death of a parent including custody arrangements, will, and so on. (13, 15)

members to attend and participate in conjoint sessions.

3. Conduct a comprehensive biopsychosocial assessment of family including when partners met, what legal relationships exist between members of family (custody, adoption, etc.), developmental milestones of children, when family first cohabitated, and any health problems in family members.

4. Assess for child abuse and report to authorities if reasonably suspected.

5. Assist client(s) in describing parenting problems in behavioral terms.

6. Ask child to describe homophobic experiences (e.g., rude comments from peers and teachers, taunting, hitting).

7. List experiences of homophobia by child and parent(s) with school officials, teachers, caregivers, and other significant people in the child's life.

8. Have the parent(s) contact the school (administrators, teachers, aides, etc.) about the homophobia being experienced by the child and develop a plan with the school to provide safety and sensitivity to child.

9. Refer child to peer support group for children of gays/lesbians.

10. Explore the specific nature of the conflicts in parenting (e.g., differences in discipline

14. Describe conflict with "in-laws" regarding raising a child. (16, 17)

15. Verbalize an understanding of how "in- laws" homophobia is negatively impacting family. (17)

16. Partners report that "in-laws" demonstrate an increased support of family (e.g., provide verbal encouragement, including client in family activities, providing childcare). (18, 19, 20)

17. Parent(s) read books/magazines that explain and support gay/lesbian families. (21)

18. Parent(s) read books on positive discipline methods for the child. (22)

19. Attend parenting classes that are sensitive to gays/ lesbians. (23)

20. Demonstrate new parenting skills in session. (22, 23, 24, 25)

21. Verbalize an understanding of how family of origin parenting roles and methods have influenced own parenting. (26)

22. Verbalize an understanding of the conflicts associated with the blending of families. (27, 28)

23. Agree about parenting roles, discipline methods, and financial arrangements. (29, 30, 31)

24. Verbalize an understanding of how internalized homophobia

methods, ability to stay home with the child).

11. Explore as to whether any economic problems may be affecting the family.

12. Probe about the effects of legal and custody problems of the child on the family.

13. Educate the client about custody issues for gay and lesbian parents and refer to a gay/ lesbian sensitive attorney for legal advice.

14. Process with family the feelings associated with the possible loss of a parent due to a life-threatening illness.

15. Discuss the impact that a life-threatening illness will have on the family. Assign family to develop and discuss a plan to take care of practical issues if the parent becomes ill.

16. Inquire about conflicts with "in-laws" regarding parenting methods.

17. Probe client(s) about how homophobic attitudes of "in-laws" negatively affect family.

18. Encourage client(s) to explain to "in- laws" how homophobic attitudes are affecting family.

19. Provide assertiveness training (e.g., making "I" statements, requesting behavioral change) and encourage client(s) to use skills with "in-laws" to establish healthy boundaries.

20. Facilitate a family therapy intervention with "in-laws,"

is contributing to anxiety about parenting. (32, 33)

25. Child identify uncomfortable feelings associated with having gay/lesbian parent(s). (34)

26. Parent explain family structure in age-appropriate terms to child. (35, 36)

27. Child read books/magazines that explain and support gay/lesbian families. (36)

28. Child list positive attributes of parents(s). (37)

29. Child describe advantages and disadvantages of growing up with gay/lesbian parent(s). (38)

30. Child describe relationships with peers and identify friends that are nonjudgmental and/or supportive of child's family. (39, 40)

31. Identify friends and/or family members willing and able to provide child care and/or emotional support. (39, 40)

32. Engage community and social support that positively supports the family structures. (41, 42)

—. _____

_____

—. _____

_____

—. _____

_____

encouraging clients to express their needs regarding child care, respect for family structure, and so on.

21. Assign client(s) to read books/magazines regarding gay/lesbian families and parenting (e.g., *The Lesbian and Gay Parenting Handbook* [Martin], *Lesbian and Gay Families: Redefining Families in America* [Pollack], *The Lesbian Parenting Book* [Clunis & Green], and *Alternative Family Magazine for Gay and Lesbian Parents and Their Children*).

22. Assign client(s) to read books about parenting methods (e.g., *The Parent's Handbook: Systematic Training for Effective Parenting* [Dinkmeyer & McKay], *The Parent's Guide* [McCarney and Bauer], *Your Child's Self-Esteem* [Briggs]). Process key points with therapist.

23. Refer client(s) to local parenting classes that are sensitive to issues faced by gays/lesbians.

24. Educate parent(s) about basic parenting skills (e.g., stages of development, discipline, child's need for consistency, self-esteem enhancement).

25. Inquire as to what clients have learned from readings and parenting classes and ask them to role play a new skill in session. Monitor for new behaviors and provide sensitive feedback.

26. Ask client(s) to describe how their parents disciplined them and what beliefs their parents had about child-rearing, noting the influence this experience has had on the client's parenting.

27. Educate client(s) about unique characteristics of blended families.

28. Explore the nature of conflicts (e.g., arguing, fighting, yelling) arising due to the blending of families.

29. Facilitate agreement between parents regarding child care expenses and income needs.

30. Using role reversal technique, have couple switch places and discuss the parenting conflict and the thoughts and feelings associated with it from each other's perspective.

31. Using a conflict resolution model, problem solve with the client(s) the roles each has or will have in the parenting of the child (e.g., who financially supports the family, who takes the child to daycare).

32. Explore client's feelings of internalized homophobia and how it may impact parenting of a child.

33. Educate client(s) regarding the facts about homosexuals in the role of parents (e.g., homosexuals are not child molesters more often than heterosexuals, studies have shown that children raised by gays or lesbians

are not any more likely to be gay or have emotional problems than children raised by heterosexuals). (See Internalized Homophobia chapter in this *Planner.*)

34. Encourage child to share uncomfortable feelings (shame, embarrassment, anger, etc.) associated with having gay/ lesbian parents.

35. Review with parents in separate session questions that child has about family structure and assist them with developing age-appropriate responses.

36. Have child read with parent(s), books *Heather Has Two Mommies* (Newman), *Jenny Lives with Eric and Martin* (Bosche), *Daddy's Roommate* (Willhoite) and *Lots of Mommies* (Severance) about having gay/lesbian parents. Discuss key points with therapist.

37. Ask child to list positive attributes of parent(s) and share in session.

38. Have child list pros and cons of growing up with gay or lesbian parents and share this list with parent(s) in session with therapist.

39. Assess child's relationship with peers including: what peers know about parent's sexuality, which friends are supportive, and conflicts with peers about parent's sexual orientation.

40. Draw an Eco-Map to assess in identifying friends and/or

family members willing and
able to provide child care
and/or emotional support.

41. Encourage client(s) to contact
reputable Internet sites, support
groups, and organizations for
gay and lesbian families (e.g.,
Family Pride Coalition, Parents
and Friends of Lesbians and
Gays, Children of Lesbians and
Gays Everywhere).

42. Have parent(s) arrange social
activities with other children of
gay/lesbian parents.

__. _____
   _____
__. _____
   _____
__. _____
   _____

DIAGNOSTIC SUGGESTIONS

Axis I:		
	309.0	Adjustment Disorder with Depressed Mood
	309.24	Adjustment Disorder with Anxiety
	309.28	Adjustment Disorder with Mixed Anxiety and Depressed Mood
	309.3	Adjustment Disorder with Disturbance of Conduct
	309.4	Adjustment Disorder with Mixed Disturbance of Emotions and Conduct
	300.4	Dysthymic Disorder
	300.02	Generalized Anxiety Disorder
	296.2	Major Depressive Disorder, Single Episode
	296.3	Major Depressive Disorder, Recurrent
	V61.20	Parent-Child Relational Problem
	_____	_____
	_____	_____

PHYSICAL ABUSE VICTIM

BEHAVIORAL DEFINITIONS

1. Confirmed self-report or account by others of verbal and/or physical assault (e.g., hitting, kicking, slapping) by partner.
2. Self-report of being injured by a domestic partner coupled with feelings of fear and/or social withdrawal.
3. Bruises or physical complaints that give evidence of assault.
4. Pronounced disturbance of mood and affect (e.g., frequent and prolonged periods of depression, irritability, anxiety and/or apathetic withdrawal).
5. Self-reported feelings of fear when in contact with domestic partner.
6. Avoidance of social activities.(e.g., work, activities with friends and/or family) due to embarrassment concerning physical bruises and other indications of assault.
7. Subjective sense of numbing, detaching, or absence of emotional responsiveness.
8. Avoidance of people and activities that remind self of the abusive relationship.
9. Difficulty sleeping, poor concentration, motor restlessness.

—. _____
_____
—. _____
_____
—. _____
_____

LONG-TERM GOALS

1. Eliminate all aggression in the relationship.
2. Establish safety plan for victim (i.e., concrete plan detailing cues for danger and steps that will be taken to enhance safety).
3. Eliminate all emotional abuse and coercion in the relationship.
4. Verbalize a plan to maintain physical and emotional safety in current and future relationships.
5. Stay away from or dramatically reduce contact with the abuser.
6. Take all legal and other steps necessary to guarantee own safety, (e.g., filing a restraining order, moving to a safe living situation, and establishing a safety plan).
7. Return to the level of emotional and social functioning present before the physical abuse began.

—. _____
   _____
—. _____
   _____
—. _____
   _____

SHORT-TERM OBJECTIVES

1. Give an accurate and emotionally honest description of the most current abuse. (1, 2, 3)

2. Identify the history, nature, frequency, and duration of abuse. (2, 3, 4)

3. Identify and express the feelings associated with the abuse (i.e., guilt, shame, helplessness). (2, 3)

4. Describe any abuse that is inflicted on others in the household. (3, 4, 5, 6)

5. Comply with a comprehensive physical evaluation to assure

THERAPEUTIC INTERVENTIONS

1. Actively build the level of trust with the client in individual sessions through consistent eye contact, active listening, unconditional positive regard, and warm acceptance to help increase his/her ability to identify and express feelings.

2. Encourage and support the client in verbally expressing and clarifying his/her perception of the facts associated with the physical abuse.

3. Explore client's feelings associated with the abuse including

that no serious injuries have been sustained and/or are untreated. (7)

6. Cooperate with a psychological evaluation. (8, 9)

7. Verbalize how abuse has impacted functioning in social, work, and family situations. (10, 11, 12, 13)

8. Identify any pattern of blaming self for the abusive behavior of the partner. (11, 13)

9. Terminate self-blame for the abuse and place responsibility on the perpetrator. (11, 13)

10. Identify those friends and family members who are understanding and supportive. (14, 17)

11. Reveal the details of the physical abuse to a friend or family member. (15)

12. Move to a safe living situation. (16, 17)

13. Write a safety plan detailing concrete actions (e.g., calling the police, leaving his/her residence, moving to a shelter) that will be taken to establish and maintain physical safety. (16, 17, 18)

14. File a restraining order. (19, 20)

15. Attend victim support groups that are sensitive to gay and lesbian domestic violence. (21, 22)

16. Read books regarding lesbian and/or gay domestic

those of guilt, shame, and/or self-blame.

4. Gather a history of physical abuse that has been endured or witnessed in the current and previous relationships.

5. Explore whether any other member of the client's current household has also been abused and, if a risk still exists, notify authorities as appropriate.

6. Inquire as to client's and other household member's safety in each session.

7. Refer client to physician for a physical exam.

8. Administer appropriate psychological tests (i.e., WAIS-R, Trail Making, MMPI) to assist with identifying any psychopathology and ruling out any neurological damage from abuse.

9. Discuss results of psychological testing and develop appropriate goals based on results.

10. Assist client in identifying the negative impact that the physical abuse has had on client's functioning at work and in social or family interactions.

11. Confront the client about making excuses for the perpetrator's abuse, minimizing its impact, or accepting blame for it.

12. Confront and challenge denial regarding the seriousness of the abuse.

violence to increase self-understanding. (23)

17. Identify the similarity between homosexual and heterosexual domestic violence. (23, 24)

18. Verbalize an understanding of how distorted beliefs have contributed to toleration of verbal and/or physical abuse. (23, 24, 25)

19. Describe any role that substance abuse may play in the role of violence. (26, 27)

20. Identify childhood experiences that taught him/her that abusive behavior is to be expected, excused, and tolerated. (28, 29)

21. List behaviors that are potential indicators of impending domestic violence in order to help prevent future episodes. (30)

22. List all behaviors that, if demonstrated by any partner, will result in immediate termination of the relationship. (30, 31)

23. Verbalize a plan for future relationships that include safety precautions. (30, 31, 32, 33)

24. Demonstrate the implementation of assertive boundary maintenance through role-playing potentially abusive situations. (34)

25. Verbalize decisions about social activities (e.g., work, living arrangements, friendships) without reference to being manipulated by abusing/controlling partner. (33, 35, 36)

13. Educate the client regarding internalization of blame.

14. Assist client in identifying friends and/or family that would be supportive of client and encourage client to seek their support.

15. Have client reveal the severity of abuse to friend or family member in session to decrease denial and increase social support.

16. Educate client about alternate living situations (e.g., domestic violence shelter, homeless shelter) that are sensitive to gays and lesbians and include them as options in a written safety plan.

17. Assist client with identifying friends or family who would be willing and able to provide a safe living situation and include them in a written safety plan.

18. Develop a written safety plan for and with client, asking him/her to sign it as part of a commitment to implement the plan when/if necessary.

19. Educate client about appropriate legal resources (e.g., district attorney, legal aid, and legal assistance from local gay and lesbian community services center).

20. Discuss with client the importance of having a restraining order in place to assure his/her safety and encourage him/her to file one.

26. Report a decreased level of fear and anxiety about future relationships. (33, 36, 37)

27. Resume previous level of social activities. (14, 21, 35, 37)

—. _____
_____

—. _____
_____

—. _____
_____

21. Educate client about domestic violence support groups that are sensitive to gays and lesbians and encourage his/her attendance.

22. Review with client his/her experience in domestic violence support group.

23. Suggest the client read books about gay or lesbian domestic violence (e.g., *Men Who Beat the Men Who Love Them* [Island & Letellier] or *Naming the Violence* [Lobell]).

24. Educate client about the cycle of domestic violence (e.g., tension-building stage, battering episode, and honeymoon stage) that occurs in heterosexual as well as homosexual relationships.

25. Assist client in identifying distorted core beliefs about homosexual relationships that perpetuate violence (e.g., "It is all right for men to hit men," or "Women can't be batterers.").

26. Gather a history of alcohol and/or drug use that occurs before, during, or after violent episodes.

27. Confront minimization of the impact of alcohol and/or drug use on domestic violence.

28. Assist client in identifying childhood events that taught him/her to excuse violent behavior.

29. Assist client in drawing a genogram indicating family

relationships of which he/she is aware were violent.

30. Review behaviors that are potential indicators of impending domestic violence (e.g., extreme jealousy, name calling, belittling, shaming).

31. Suggest that client list all behaviors (e.g., threatening physical violence, hitting, slapping) that, if present in any partner, would be cause for immediate termination of the relationship.

32. Assist client with developing a plan for future relationships that includes safety precautions.

33. Explore fear and anxiety about future relationships.

34. Provide assertiveness training emphasizing the maintenance of physical safety boundaries and role play with him/her the application of assertiveness in potentially abusive situations.

35. Monitor progress toward increased social activity and positively reinforce movement toward that goal.

36. Assist client in identifying irrational fears regarding being re-victimized and replacing those fears with more rational beliefs.

37. Have client write a "future" biography describing his/her life after the emotional effects of the abuse have been resolved to

assist him/her with establishing long-term relationship goals.

___. _____
   _____
___. _____
   _____
___. _____
   _____

DIAGNOSTIC SUGGESTIONS

Axis I:	308.3	Acute Stress Disorder
	309.0	Adjustment Disorder with Depressed Mood
	309.24	Adjustment Disorder with Anxiety
	309.28	Adjustment Disorder with Mixed Anxiety and Depressed Mood
	305.00	Alcohol Abuse
	303.90	Alcohol Dependence
	300.4	Dysthymic Disorder
	296.xx	Major Depressive Disorder
	V61.1	Partner Relational Problem
	995.81	Physical Abuse of Adult (If Focus of Clinical Attention Is on the Victim)
	309.81	Posttraumatic Stress Disorder
	_____	_____
	_____	_____
Axis II:	301.83	Borderline Personality Disorder
	301.6	Dependent Personality Disorder
	301.50	Histrionic Personality Disorder
	_____	_____
	_____	_____

RELIGIOUS CONFLICTS

BEHAVIORAL DEFINITIONS

1. Belief that homosexuality and religious/spiritual involvement are mutually exclusive.
2. Expressing shame over homosexual behavior and/or desires because of fear of God's condemnation.
3. Avoidance of spiritual activities in spite of deeply held spiritual beliefs.
4. Increasingly negative emotional reactions (e.g., anger, depression, isolation) to current religious group because of its condemnation of homosexuality.
5. Frustration with the perceived inability to disclose sexual orientation to religious group (e.g., priest, rabbi, minister, congregation).
6. Desire to consecrate relationship with partner in a religious commitment ceremony.
7. Unable to articulate a concept of Higher Power and/or God which is accepting of homosexuality.
8. Recent "failure" of reparative therapy which has increased client's feelings of shame, hopelessness, and self-loathing.
9. Difficulty participating in 12-Step group (e.g., Alcoholics Anonymous, Sexual Compulsives Anonymous) because of spiritual component.

___. _____
_____
___. _____
_____
___. _____
_____

LONG-TERM GOALS

1. Resolve conflict between religious beliefs and homosexual identity by modifying belief system.
2. Develop a personal definition of spirituality which is accepting and supportive of homosexual identity.
3. Believe that God/Higher Power loves and accepts self.
4. Eliminate any sense of shame or guilt because of conflict between homosexual behavior and religious beliefs.
5. Report that religious/spiritual beliefs are a constant source of support and reassurance.
6. Participate in religious/spiritual activities and communities which are supportive of lesbians/gay men.
7. Increased inner experience of calm, peace, and serenity.

—. _____
_____
—. _____
_____
—. _____
_____

SHORT-TERM OBJECTIVES	THERAPEUTIC INTERVENTIONS
1. Openly describe the emotional reactions to conflict between homosexual identity and practice and religious/spiritual beliefs. (1)	1. Actively build the level of trust with the client in individual sessions through consistent eye contact, active listening, unconditional positive regard, and warm acceptance to help increase his/her ability to identify and express feelings.
2. Discuss messages from childhood religious experiences that condemned homosexuality. (2, 3)	2. Explore client's childhood experience with being taught that homosexual thoughts, feelings, and/or behavior are condemned by God.
3. Verbalize an understanding of how childhood experiences and relationships have influenced concept of God/Higher Power. (2, 3)	3. Confront client with similarity between parental/authority figure relationships from child-
4. Identify cognitive distortions that are contributing to conflict	

and replace with more realistic, positive messages. (4)

5. List 10 qualities of a moral person and relate these to own homosexual identity. (5)

6. Verbalize an understanding of current knowledge of homosexuality. (6)

7. Read books which describe spiritual/religious conflicts among lesbians and gay men. (7)

8. Read books which provide information about history of religion and homosexuality. (8)

9. Watch movies/videos that depict spiritual conflicts among lesbians and gay men. (9)

10. Verbalize an understanding of the 12-Step concept of Higher Power. (10)

11. Write a description of what client believes God or a Higher Power must be. (11)

12. Identify religious/spiritual groups which are supportive of lesbians and gay men. (12)

13. Attend religious/spiritual groups which are supportive of gay men and lesbians. (13)

14. Interview other gay men and lesbians about their spiritual/religious beliefs. (14)

15. Find a religious leader willing to preside over commitment ceremony. (15)

16. Verbalize an understanding of meditation techniques and report their use. (16, 17)

hood (e.g., authoritative, judgmental father) and concept of God/Higher Power (e.g., authoritative, judgmental God).

4. Assist client in identifying cognitive distortions about spirituality that contribute to conflict (e.g., all religions condemn homosexuality, or no church would accept an openly gay/lesbian person) and replacing them with more realistic beliefs (e.g., some religious people condemn homosexuality, but others are accepting, or there are religious groups that accept homosexual members).

5. Assign client homework of listing 10 qualities of a moral person (e.g., a moral person is kind and compassionate, a moral person does not intentionally hurt others). Ask client if his/her definition of morality in any way conflicts with his/her homosexuality. Process reaction in session.

6. Educate client about homosexuality (e.g., research indicates that homosexuality is probably not a choice but an inherited trait, and typically can not be "reversed" through reparative therapy).

7. Assign client to read books that describe spiritual/religious conflicts among lesbians and gay men (e.g., *Oranges Are Not the Only Fruit* [Winterson], *Stranger at the Gate* [White], *Freedom, Glorious Freedom*

17. Attend yoga group. (18)

18. Keep a journal of experiences of times of feeling closest to God and/or spirituality. (19)

19. Participate in experiences that increase subjective sense of closeness to God and/or spirituality. (19, 20)

—. _____
_____
—. _____
_____
—. _____
_____

[McNeill]). Process reactions in session.

8. Assign client to read Boswell's *Christianity, Social Tolerance and Homosexuality.* Process reactions in session.

9. Assign client homework of watching videos/films that depict religious conflict among gay men and lesbians (e.g., *All God's Children* or *One Nation Under God*).

10. Educate the client about the 12-Step concept of Higher Power (i.e., the personal concept of a Higher Power, not one derived from external sources).

11. Assign client homework of describing his/her understanding of God/Higher Power (e.g., God is love, God is just, God is forgiving). Probe regarding conflict between client's concept of God and homosexuality.

12. Educate client about the existence of religious/spiritual groups which are supportive of lesbians and gay men (e.g, Affirmation for Mormons, Dignity for Catholics, Integrity for Episcopalians, Metropolitan Community Church, Lutherans Concerned, and gay Zen groups).

13. Encourage client to attend a supportive spiritual/religious group of his/her choice. Process reactions in session.

14. Assign client homework of interviewing other gay men

and/or lesbians to ask them specific questions about their spiritual/religious beliefs (e.g., What do you believe God/ Higher Power is? How do you reconcile being a feminist with a patriarchal religion? Do you believe God condemns homo-sexuality?). Process reactions in session.

15. Have client contact lesbian/gay friendly religious groups to lo-cate leader willing to preside over commitment ceremony.

16. Educate client about meditation techniques (e.g, counting breaths, clearing thoughts) and encourage him/her to explore them.

17. Refer client to meditation group.

18. Refer client to yoga group.

19. Assign client homework of keeping journal of recording experiences during which he/ she felt closest to God and/or spirituality (e.g., walks in nature, talking with family, meditating, praying, reading devotional material, attending synagogue/church).

20. Encourage client to increase frequency of participation in experiences that increase feel-ings of closeness to God and/or spirituality.

___. _____
   _____
___. _____
   _____
   _____
___. _____
   _____

DIAGNOSTIC SUGGESTIONS

Axis I:	309.0	Adjustment Disorder with Depressed Mood
	309.24	Adjustment Disorder with Anxiety
	309.28	Adjustment Disorder with Mixed Anxiety and Depressed Mood
	300.4	Dysthymic Disorder
	296.xx	Major Depressive Disorder
	_____	_____
	_____	_____

SAFER SEX

BEHAVIORAL DEFINITIONS

1. Lack of awareness regarding means of avoiding transmission of HIV.
2. Concern of infecting HIV negative partner.
3. Intermittent "relapse" into high risk sexual behaviors.
4. Little or no desire for sexual activity.
5. Recurrent lack of usual physiological response of sexual excitement and arousal (genital lubrication and swelling).

—. _____
   _____
—. _____
   _____
   _____
—. _____
   _____

LONG-TERM GOALS

1. Awareness of safer sex practices.
2. Elimination of high-risk sexual behaviors.
3. Increase desire for and enjoyment of sexual activities.
4. Engage in a range of sexual activities that are a source of pleasure.

—. _____
   _____
—. _____
   _____
   _____
—. _____
   _____

SHORT-TERM OBJECTIVES

1. Openly describe current sexual practices. (1)

2. List no-risk sexual behaviors. (2)

3. List low-risk sexual behaviors. (3)

4. List high-risk sexual behaviors. (4)

5. Identify all sexual behaviors which increase risk for HIV infection. (3, 4, 5)

6. Get a blood test for HIV. (6)

7. Express emotional reactions to waiting for results from HIV test. (7, 8)

8. Verbalize an understanding of how substance abuse increases risk of contracting HIV. (9)

9. Abstain from drug and alcohol use prior to sexual activity. (10, 11)

10. Attend 12-Step group to maintain abstinence from drugs and alcohol. (12)

11. Demonstrate proper use of condoms. (13)

12. Develop a plan for avoiding HIV infection. (14)

13. Role play assertively insisting on safer sex boundaries with sexual partners. (15, 16)

14. Identify any automatic thoughts of beliefs that contribute to unsafe sexual behaviors. (17)

15. Verbalize frustrations with safer sex guidelines. (18)

THERAPEUTIC INTERVENTIONS

1. Conduct an assessment of client's current sexual practices including with whom sex is shared, under what circumstances, and when safer sex practices are not followed.

2. Assist client in listing no-risk sexual activities (e.g., individual masturbation, massage, phone sex, showering with another person).

3. Assist client in listing low-risk sexual behaviors (e.g., fellatio with no exchange of semen, intercourse with condom).

4. Assist client in identifying and listing high risk behaviors (e.g., intercourse without a condom, cunnilingus without a barrier).

5. Assist client in identifying sexual practices that put him/her at risk for HIV infection.

6. Refer client to site for anonymous HIV testing (e.g., AIDS Project, public health clinic) or encourage him/her to use home test kit for HIV.

7. Process emotional reactions to waiting for HIV results.

8. Assign client to write a journal of fears, anxiety, dread, and so on that he/she feels while waiting for test results. Process with therapist.

9. Explore substance abuse as an escape from stress, physical, and emotional pain and

16. Verbalize an understanding of how high risk sexual activity has been used to cope with negative emotions (e.g., anxiety, depression, loneliness). (19, 20)

17. List alternative coping strategies to deal with negative emotions. (21)

18. Practice relaxation techniques. (22)

19. Identify ways that sexual activities could be enhanced to provide more satisfaction. (23)

20. Attend a workshop on eroticizing safer sex. (24)

21. Attend HIV negative support group. (25)

22. Volunteer at AIDS project to increase knowledge of HIV disease and decrease denial about living with HIV disease. (26)

—. _____
_____
—. _____
_____
—. _____
_____

boredom; confront the negative consequences of this pattern of behavior.

10. Educate client how substance abuse prior to or during sex increases likelihood of HIV transmission (e.g., less likely to follow safer sex guidelines, more impulsive about sexuality).

11. Press for commitment to abstain from drugs and alcohol prior to sexual activity and refer for treatment or treat for chemical dependence. (See Chemical Dependence chapter in this *Planner*.)

12. Refer to 12-Step group (e.g., AA, NA) to provide support for abstinence from drugs and alcohol.

13. Have client demonstrate the proper use of condoms by enveloping a banana, dildo, or other item.

14. Assist client in developing a plan to avoid HIV infection (e.g., abstaining from drugs and alcohol before sex, eliminating high risk sexual behaviors).

15. Train client in assertiveness skills.

16. Have client role play difficult situations where partner insists upon high risk sexual activity and client maintains sexual boundaries (e.g., partner requests sex without condom and client refuses).

17. Assist client in identifying any automatic thoughts that contribute to high-risk sexual behaviors (e.g., "This guy looks too healthy to be infected," or "I don't enjoy sex with condoms") and replace with more realistic thoughts that reinforce safer sex guidelines (e.g., "You can't tell if someone is infected by the way they look," "I enjoy some safer sex and really would hate being infected with HIV").

18. Probe client about frustrations with safer sex guidelines (e.g., they're not as spontaneous, enjoyable, intimate, etc.).

19. Explore whether high-risk sexual activity has been used to cope with negative emotions (e.g., loneliness, boredom, anxiety) by reviewing with client mood state before sexual activity.

20. Assign client homework of keeping mood record throughout the week. Focus upon any negative emotions experienced prior to high-risk sexual activity.

21. Have client list alternative coping strategies (e.g., calling friends when lonely, practicing relaxation techniques when anxious, exercising) to deal with negative emotions.

22. Teach client relaxation techniques (e.g., deep breathing, meditation, muscle relaxation).

23. Educate client(s) about the use of sexual aids (e.g., lesbian erotica, vibrators, lotions) that may increase sexual pleasure.

24. Refer to group that teaches safer sex practices and ways to eroticize safer sex (e.g., groups at local AIDS project or gay and lesbian community center).

25. Refer to HIV negative support group to increase commitment to stay uninfected.

26. Encourage client to volunteer at AIDS project.

—. _____
   _____
—. _____
   _____
—. _____
   _____

DIAGNOSTIC SUGGESTIONS

Axis I:	296.2x	Major Depressive Disorder, Single Episode
	296.3x	Major Depressive Disorder, Recurrent
	300.02	Generalized Anxiety Disorder
	316	Maladaptive Health Behaviors Affecting . . . [Indicate the General Medical Condition]
	309.0	Adjustment Disorder with Depressed Mood
	300.4	Dysthymic Disorder
	309.24	Adjustment Disorder with Anxiety
	309.28	Adjustment Disorder with Mixed Anxiety and Depressed Mood
	_____	_____
	_____	_____
Axis II:	301.7	Antisocial Personality Disorder
	301.83	Borderline Personality Disorder
	301.81	Narcissistic Personality Disorder
	_____	_____
	_____	_____

SEPARATION

BEHAVIORAL DEFINITIONS

1. Recent separation from an intimate partner.
2. Considering a separation from partner but experiencing ambivalence.
3. Fear and anxiety about living life after separation as a single person.
4. Anger about partner's infidelity that led to separation.
5. Feelings of fear, loneliness, loss, and isolation.
6. Arguments resulting from division of property.
7. Conflicts regarding custody of children.
8. Child's persistent, excessive worry about separation from parent.
9. Feelings of low self-worth and guilt over perceived failures that contributed to the separation.

—. _____
   _____
   _____
—. _____
   _____
   _____
—. _____
   _____

LONG-TERM GOALS

1. Grieve loss experienced due to separation and develop a renewed sense of well being.
2. Accept termination of the relationship and the change it has brought about in life.
3. Make a healthy transition into new role as a single person.
4. Develop a sense of confidence about choice to separate.
5. Increase awareness of own role in the relationship conflicts.
6. Resolve angry feelings about partner's infidelity.
7. Develop new friendships with people with like interests.

8. Fairly divide property through negotiation and compromise.
9. Develop and accept a coparenting plan that is fair and equitable and is in the best interests of the child(ren).
10. Resolve feelings of low self-worth and guilt over selection of partner and uncover self-defeating behaviors to avoid problems in future relationships.

—. _____
   _____
   _____

—. _____
   _____
   _____

—. _____
   _____

SHORT-TERM OBJECTIVES	THERAPEUTIC INTERVENTIONS
1. Describe current status of relationship honestly and openly. (1)	1. Actively build level of trust with the client(s) to help them identify and express feelings associated with separation.
2. Share facts and feelings that have led to the separation. (2)	2. Have client(s) describe history of relationship and facts that have led to separation or termination of relationship, including client assessing own role in the relationship conflict.
3. Identify any verbal, physical, and/or sexual abuse in the relationship. (3)	3. Probe client regarding any verbal, physical, and/or sexual abuse in the relationship. Develop safety plan if abuse exists. (See Physical Abuse Victim chapter in this *Planner.*)
4. Verbalize emotions associated with making choice to separate. (4, 5)	4. Explore feelings of fear, anger, ambivalence, and grief associated with separation.
5. Identify emotional impact of infidelity on relationship. (5)	5. Explore the feelings (anger, rage, depression, betrayal, etc.) associated with infidelity in the
6. Discuss family of origin relationships to increase awareness of interpersonal dynamics. (6, 7)	
7. Verbalize an understanding of how a family history of broken committed relationships have an impact on decision to separate. (6, 7)	

8. List pros and cons of remaining in the relationship. (8)

9. List pros and cons of terminating the relationship. (9)

10. Make a decision to continue with the relationship or terminate it. (8, 9, 10)

11. State date when one partner will move out. (10)

12. Verbalize an understanding the impact separation will have on social life, family, and so on, and develop a tentative plan to adapt to the changes. (11)

13. Write a separation plan that details future contact, child custody agreements, property distribution, and so on. (12, 13, 14, 15)

14. Verbalize a commitment of sensitivity to the children's feelings and needs during the time of separation. (16, 17)

15. Agree about way in which to tell children about separation. (18)

16. Bring children into sessions to express feelings and needs. (19)

17. Develop a co-parenting agreement that takes into account the children's emotional, financial, and custody concerns. (20, 21, 22)

18. Discuss feelings associated with return to dating. (23)

19. Verbalize the feeling of a loss associated with the separation. (24, 25)

relationship. (See Intimate Relationship Conflicts chapter in this *Planner.*)

6. Probe each client about family of origin history to see if interactional patterns of destructive intimate relationships are repeating themselves in the present relationship.

7. Probe client(s) about family of origin relationships and how his/her history of broken committed relationships have impact on current decision to separate.

8. Have client(s) list pros and cons of remaining in the relationship. Process list in session with therapist.

9. Review with client(s) reasons for and against termination of relationship and wish to separate.

10. Encourage client to set a date by which decision to stay in relationship or terminate it will be made.

11. Probe each client about the impact the separation will have on social life, family, financial situation, and so on. Encourage client(s) to identify plans (e.g., see friends more often, attend support group, begin individual therapy) to adapt to changes.

12. Assist client(s) in negotiating the terms and conditions relating to the termination of the relationship. Process any conflicts in session with therapist.

20. Read books on lesbian and gay relationships to increase knowledge of dysfunctional patterns to prevent recurrence in new relationships. (26)

21. Attend a single parent support group. (27)

22. Develop a plan to increase social activities and strengthen social support system. (28, 29, 30)

23. Report increased social activity. (28, 29, 31)

24. Verbalize an understanding of safer sex practices and report their use in new relationships. (32, 33)

——. _____
   _____
——. _____
   _____
——. _____
   _____

13. Have client(s) list terms and conditions regarding the termination of the relationship and the nature of future contact.

14. Probe client(s) about feelings associated with the division of property.

15. Have client(s) write a list of property shared in common and develop a plan to divide property.

16. Educate client(s) about the impact of separation upon children. Confront any minimization of children's needs during session.

17. Press for commitment to consider best interests of children throughout separation process.

18. Assist client(s) in finding ways to tell children about impending separation and its impact on their lives. Have client(s) agree about content, time, and place to tell the children of impending termination of the relationship.

19. Encourage client(s) to bring children into sessions to express feelings and needs.

20. Assist client(s) in developing a co-parenting agreement which provides for children's emotional, financial, and custody concerns.

21. Facilitate agreement between parents regarding co-parenting procedures.

22. Refer client(s) to lesbian/gay sensitive legal counsel to assist in custody issues.

23. Explore feelings associated with a new identity as a single person.

24. Explore feelings associated with the losses (life as a couple, financial, belongings, standing in the community, etc.) resulting from termination of the relationship.

25. Assign client to read *How to Survive the Loss of a Love* (Colgrove, Bloomfield, & McWillams) and process key concepts with therapist.

26. Assign client(s) to read selected passages in books focusing on lesbian/gay relationships (e.g., *The Intimacy Dance* [Berzon], *The Lesbian & Gay Book of Love & Marriage* [Martinac], *Lesbian Couples* [Clunis & Green], *Permanent Partners* [Berzon]). Process key ideas with therapist.

27. Refer client(s) to single parent support group which is oriented toward gays/lesbians, if available.

28. Assist client(s) in identifying activities he/she would find pleasurable and encourage participation in these activities.

29. Refer client(s) to lesbian/gay oriented social activities (gay running clubs, food clubs, etc.) and encourage participation.

30. Assist client in developing a specific plan regarding building new social relationships to overcome withdrawal and fear of rejection.

31. Monitor progress toward increased social activity and positively reinforce movement toward that goal.

32. Discuss safer sex techniques and encourage use in future sexual relations.

33. Review with client negotiation of sexual activity and assertiveness skills for future relationships.

___. _____

_____

___. _____

_____

___. _____

_____

DIAGNOSTIC SUGGESTIONS

Axis I:	296.xx	Major Depressive Disorder
	309.0	Adjustment Disorder with Depressed Mood
	309.24	Adjustment Disorder with Anxiety
	309.28	Adjustment Disorder with Mixed Anxiety and Depressed Mood
	309.4	Adjustment Disorder with Mixed Disturbance of Emotions and Conduct
	300.4	Dysthymic Disorder
	300.02	Generalized Anxiety Disorder
	V61.1	Partner Relational Problem
	309.21	Separation Anxiety Disorder
	_____	_____
	_____	_____

Axis II:	301.83	Borderline Personality Disorder
	301.6	Dependent Personality Disorder
	301.5	Histrionic Personality Disorder
	301.81	Narcissistic Personality Disorder
	_____	_____
	_____	_____

SEXUAL ABUSE

BEHAVIORAL DEFINITIONS

1. Vague memories of inappropriate childhood sexual contact that can be corroborated by significant others.
2. Self-report of being sexually abused with clear, detailed memories.
3. Blaming childhood sexual abuse on characteristics of self (e.g., being gay/lesbian, being promiscuous, effeminate/masculine, "wanting" homosexual experience).
4. A pattern of self-injurious behavior (e.g., burning, cutting, or scratching skin).
5. Intrusive memories, disturbing recollections, and/or nightmares of childhood sexual abuse.
6. Self-report of feelings of helplessness, hopelessness, and/or anxiety.
7. A pattern of difficulties in performing and/or enjoying sexual activities.
8. Avoidance of activities, situations, and/or people that remind client of abuse.
9. A pattern of difficulty maintaining intimate relationships because of anxiety, fear, and helplessness related to childhood sexual abuse.
10. Restricted range of affect.
11. Subjective sense of numbing, detaching, or absence of emotional responsiveness.
12. Difficulty sleeping, poor concentration, motor restlessness.

___. _____
   _____
___. _____
   _____
___. _____
   _____

LONG-TERM GOALS

1. Reduce frequency of intrusive memories, nightmares, and recollections of abuse.
2. Place responsibility for abuse on the perpetrator.
3. Eliminate any self-injurious behavior.
4. Engage in sexual activities which are a source of satisfaction and do not pose a threat to client's physical, social, or psychological well-being.
5. Engage in a broad variety of rewarding social activities.

___. _____
     _____
___. _____
     _____
___. _____
     _____

SHORT-TERM OBJECTIVES

1. Cooperate with comprehensive biopsychosocial assessment by honestly sharing facts related to the sexual abuse. (1)

2. Openly express emotional re-actions (e.g, shame, guilt, anxiety, fear) to sexual abuse. (2, 3)

3. Identify any obstacles to feeling safe in relationship with therapist and establish therapeutic pace that is comfortable. (2, 3)

4. Verbalize an understanding of the boundaries of therapeutic relationship. (4)

5. Cooperate with assessment for suicidality and depression. (5, 6)

THERAPEUTIC INTERVENTIONS

1. Conduct a comprehensive bio-psychosocial assessment of client including focusing on specifics of abuse including client's age at the time of abuse, relationship to abuser, frequency of abuse, and re-sponse of social support/family to abuse.

2. Establish working relationship with client by inquiring about emotional reactions, providing empathetic responses, taking a nonjudgmental stance, and so on.

3. Educate client about how sex-ual abuse affects victims' abil-ity to trust and encourage him/her to proceed at a pace of self-disclosure that is comfortable

6. Cooperate with standardized psychological testing to determine severity of symptoms and social impairment. (6)

7. Accept referral to a physician for psychotropic medication evaluation. (5, 6)

8. Take medication as prescribed by physician and report as to effectiveness and side effects. (7)

9. Identify any self-injurious behaviors (e.g., cutting, burning). (8)

10. Sign a no-harm contract. (9)

11. List five alternatives to engaging in self-injurious behavior. (10)

12. Identify any verbal, physical, and/or sexual abuse in current relationships. (11)

13. Partner agrees to participate in conjoint sessions with client. (12)

14. Partner identifies problems in the relationship because of client's sexual abuse. (13, 14)

15. Partner verbalizes understanding of and support for client. (15)

16. Identify any cognitive distortions that contribute to blaming self for the sexual abuse and replace with more realistic beliefs. (16)

17. Terminate self-blame for the abuse and place responsibility on the perpetrator. (16, 17)

18. Identify any cognitive distortions related to being

and to notify therapist when feeling unsafe.

4. Review therapeutic framework with client including length of sessions, fee arrangements, calls between sessions, and prohibition of dual relationships.

5. Assess client for signs and symptoms of depression and suicidality; referring to psychiatrist for medications if indicated. (See Depression chapter in this *Planner*.)

6. Administer the *Beck Depression Inventory* (Beck) *Clinician-Administered PTSD Scale* (CAPS, [Blake et al.]) and/or the *PTSD Symptom Scale* (PSS, [Foa et al.]) to assist with diagnosis and to determine the severity of symptoms and impairment.

7. Monitor client's medication prescription compliance assessing effectiveness and side effects.

8. Assess whether or not client is engaging in any self-injurious behaviors by asking him/her directly.

9. Encourage client to sign a no-harm contract specifying which behaviors are to be prohibited (e.g., cutting wrists, taking medications in amounts greater than prescribed) and consequences for not complying with contract (e.g., admission to inpatient treatment before

homosexual and being abused and replace with realistic beliefs. (16, 17, 18)

19. Write a letter to the abuser. (19)

20. Read books on childhood sexual abuse. (20)

21. Attend support groups for survivors of child sexual abuse that are sensitive to the needs of lesbian and gay men. (21)

22. Practice slow, deep breathing to decrease anxiety. (22)

23. Demonstrate the ability to quantify distress by using Subjective Units of Distress (SUDs). (23)

24. List situations, places, and people that are being avoided. (24, 25)

25. Arrange the avoided situations into an anxiety hierarchy. (26)

26. Practice imaginal systematic desensitization exposure to anxiety-producing elements of the abuse to reduce fear, anxiety, and dissociation. (27, 28)

27. Confront avoided situations with a supportive friend, partner, or family member. (13, 29, 30)

28. Verbalize an increased sense of well-being. (31)

—. _____
  _____
—. _____
  _____
—. _____
  _____

therapy continues, notification of significant others).

10. Assign client homework of listing five alternatives to self-injurious behavior (e.g., taking a walk, writing in a journal, talking to a friend) and encourage him/her to utilize these when feeling anxious, depressed and so on.

11. Assess for any verbal, physical, and/or sexual abuse in current relationships.

12. Encourage client to include partner in conjoint sessions to facilitate conflict resolution and increase client's social support.

13. Educate client's partner about the effects of childhood sexual abuse on self-esteem and on relationships.

14. Ask partner to describe any problems in relationship because of sexual abuse (e.g., little or no sexual activity, problems with client meeting parental obligations.)

15. Have client describe to partner what he/she needs to feel supported and safe in relationship. (See Intimate Relationship Conflicts chapter in this *Planner*.)

16. Probe client for cognitive distortions that contribute to blaming self for the abuse (e.g., "I didn't fight back so I must have wanted it." "My father was a good man so there must have been something bad about

me") and assist him/her in replacing with more realistic beliefs (e.g., "I was too young to defend myself." "My father was a good parent in some areas, but he molested me because something was wrong with him, not me").

17. Confront client regarding self-blame and assist client in placing responsibility for victimization on the perpetrator.

18. Provide client with examples of common faulty beliefs gay and lesbian survivors of abuse have about being abused (e.g., "Being abused made me gay/lesbian," "It wasn't abuse because I 'wanted' it") and assist him/her in replacing with more realistic beliefs (e.g., "There's no evidence that sexual abuse affects sexual orientation," Sex between a child and an adult is an abuse of power").

19. Assign client homework of writing a letter to the abuser and encourage him/her to express the impact abuse had on his/her life and the emotions (e.g., rage, sadness) that client feels toward abuser.

20. Assign books on childhood sexual abuse that include content on special needs of lesbian and gay survivors (e.g., *The Courage to Heal: A Guide for Women Survivors of Child Sexual Abuse* [Bass & Davis], *Victims No Longer: Men Recovering from Incest and*

Other Sexual Child Abuse
[Lew]).

21. Refer client to support groups for survivors of child sexual abuse such as Incest Survivors Anonymous, and Victims of Incest Can Emerge Survivors (VOICES) that are sensitive to the needs of lesbians and gay men.

22. Train the client in deep, abdominal breathing techniques to decrease anxiety and encourage their practice in and between sessions.

23. Educate client about the use of SUDs to rate the degree of anxiety experienced generally or in the presence of specific stimuli.

24. Provide client with examples of situations (e.g., consensual sexual activities, sleeping in a bedroom without the light on, showers) that are commonly avoided as a result of being sexually abused.

25. Ask client to list situations that he/she is avoiding due to the abuse.

26. Assist client in creating a hierarchy by his/her rating avoided situations on a scale of 1 to 100 subjective units of discomfort.

27. Conduct imaginal systematic desensitization exposure using the hierarchy of avoided events (e.g., have client describe events/situations from the hierarchy of SUDs until they have been decreased to tolerable or negligible levels).

28. Reinforce client's progress in reducing fear and avoidance by providing positive feedback and encouragement to the desensitization process.

29. Educate client's significant others about the effects of being victimized and *in vivo* exposure techniques. Enlist them in providing support as client confronts avoided situations.

30. Assign homework of *in vivo* exposure to anxiety producing stimulus situations (e.g., being able to confront avoided situations with a friend, partner, family member). Process reactions with therapist in session.

31. Review client's progress by describing his/her original level of functioning and noting changes.

___. _____

_____

___. _____

_____

___. _____

_____

DIAGNOSTIC SUGGESTIONS

Axis I:	308.3	Acute Stress Disorder
	300.12	Dissociative Amnesia
	300.14	Dissociative Identity Disorder
	300.15	Dissociative Disorder NOS
	300.4	Dysthymic Disorder
	300.02	Generalized Anxiety Disorder
	296.xx	Major Depressive Disorder
	309.81	Posttraumatic Stress Disorder
	_____	_____
	_____	_____
Axis II:	301.82	Avoidant Personality Disorder
	301.83	Borderline Personality Disorder
	301.6	Dependent Personality Disorder
	301.50	Histrionic Personality Disorder
	_____	_____
	_____	_____

SEXUAL ACTING OUT

BEHAVIORAL DEFINITIONS

1. Arrests for illegal sexual behaviors (e.g., prostitution, soliciting a police officer, indecent exposure, voyeurism, selling/buying child pornography, sexual acts with a minor).
2. Economic problems (overdue bills, bankruptcy, etc.) because of large investment of money in sexually oriented pursuits (e.g., pornography, on-line sex, phone sex, and prostitution).
3. Recurrent, intense sexually arousing fantasies, sexual urges, or behaviors that cause client distress.
4. Continued high degree of sexual activity (promiscuity) despite the verbalized desire to reduce or terminate it.
5. Continued sexual behavior(s) despite persistent physical, legal, financial, vocational, social, or relationship problems that are directly caused by the sexual behavior(s).
6. A pattern of contracting multiple sexually transmitted diseases (HIV, syphilis, chlamydia, etc.).
7. Suspension of important social, recreational, or occupational activities because they interfere with sexual activities.
8. Engaging in unprotected sex.

___. _____
   _____
___. _____
   _____
___. _____
   _____

LONG-TERM GOALS

1. Control sexual behavior and begin to actively participate in a treatment program.
2. Terminate sexual behavior that is illegal and/or leads to economic, medical, social, and relational problems.
3. Engage in sexual activities which are a source of satisfaction and do not pose a threat to client's physical, social, vocational, or psychological well-being.
4. Acquire the skills necessary to maintain behavioral changes and develop mutually satisfying sexual relationships.
5. Improve quality of life by maintaining abstinence from all illegal sexual activities.

—. _____
   _____
   _____
—. _____
   _____
   _____
—. _____
   _____
   _____

SHORT-TERM OBJECTIVES

1. Provide accurate and complete information for biopsychosocial history focusing upon sexual history. (1)

2. Cooperate with a medical examination. (2, 3)

3. Comply with medical doctor's recommendations regarding treatment for sexually transmitted diseases (STDs). (4)

4. Verbalize an awareness of safer-sex guidelines to prevent HIV infection and other STDs. (5)

5. List negative emotional, physical, spiritual, relational, and

THERAPEUTIC INTERVENTIONS

1. Gather a complete history including childhood sexual experiences, arrests, amount of time/money spent on sexual activities.

2. Refer client for thorough physical examination to determine if there are any sexually transmitted diseases (e.g, HIV/AIDS, gonorrhea, chlamydia) present.

3. Inquire as to results of physical examination and refer to specialized treatment services as needed (e.g., public health centers, AIDS projects).

occupational consequences resulting from sexual acting out. (6)

6. Verbalize an understanding of how uncontrolled sexual activity increases the risk of contracting HIV and other sexually transmitted diseases. (2, 5, 7)

7. Agree to abstain from all sexual activities for six weeks. (8)

8. Identify the ways controlling sexual impulses could positively impact life. (9)

9. Read assigned material to increase knowledge of the concept of sexual addiction. (10)

10. Verbalize an increased knowledge of 12-Step approaches to changing sexual behavior. (10, 11, 12)

11. Identify community resources that are supportive of gay men and lesbians changing their sexual behavior. (11, 12)

12. Attend a self-help group to support efforts to decrease sexual compulsivity. (11, 12)

13. List 10 sexual activities that do not cause the client or anyone else distress, are a source of pleasure and satisfaction, and are in harmony with societal laws and personal moral/spiritual values. (10, 11, 13)

14. List sexual activities that are considered appropriate and inappropriate. (14)

4. Inquire about compliance with medical recommendations and confront any avoidance of seeking appropriate medical care.

5. Teach details of safer sex guidelines and encourage client to include them in all future sexual activity.

6. Ask client to list all negative consequences of sexual acting out.

7. Educate the client about his/her higher risk of contracting HIV and other sexually transmitted diseases because of lack of control over sexual impulses.

8. Ask client to abstain from all sexual activities for six weeks to determine how difficult it is to control sexual impulses and to identify appropriate versus inappropriate sexual activities.

9. Ask the client how his/her life would be improved if he/she were not engaged in sexual acting out.

10. Ask the client to read books that provide information about 12-Step approach to sexual addiction and recovery (e.g., *Out of the Shadows: Understanding Sexual Addiction* [Carnes]).

11. Refer to Sexual Compulsives Anonymous (SCA) or another 12-Step group; encourage and reinforce consistent attendance.

12. Assign client to meet with a gay/lesbian member of Sexual

15. Write a sexual behavior plan in concrete, behavioral terms. (15)

16. Identify childhood experiences that have contributed to sexual acting out. (16, 17, 18, 19)

17. Verbalize a resolution of feelings regarding sexual trauma or abuse experiences. (16, 18, 19)

18. List the negative emotions that were caused or exacerbated by a lack of control over sexual impulses. (20)

19. Verbalize areas of sexual behavior plan that are particularly difficult to maintain. (21, 22)

20. List coping skills necessary to overcome triggers to sexual acting out. (22, 23)

21. Identify rituals that preceded sexual acting out. (24)

22. Verbalize a plan to terminate rituals that precede acting out. (25)

23. List all lies used to hide inappropriate sexual behavior. (26)

24. Identify pleasurable activities that will assist in maintaining sexual behavioral changes. (27)

25. Practice stress management skills to reduce overall stress levels, relax, and feel comfortable. (28)

26. List 10 distraction behaviors to use to cope with sexual urges and craving that could lead to engaging in sexually compulsive behaviors. (29)

Compulsives Anonymous who has maintained sexual abstinence for several years and find out specifically how the program has helped him/her stay sober.

13. Assign client homework of listing 10 sexual activities that are a source of pleasure and satisfaction which are in accord with societal laws, personal moral/spiritual code of values and cause no harm to self or others.

14. Assign client homework of listing appropriate and inappropriate sexual behaviors.

15. Assign client to write a sexual behavior plan including goals (e.g., "I will not buy any sexually oriented magazines," "I won't have any sexual contact with a person until at least the third date," "I won't go into the adult section of the bookstore or video store") and ways to attain them (e.g., attend SCA three times a week, individual therapy once a week).

16. Assign client homework of writing a biography detailing sexual experiences and messages from childhood. Discuss in session.

17. Explore for modeling effects within the extended family by drawing a genogram especially highlighting any unhealthy sexual behavior of family members which crossed over boundaries of propriety. Process reactions with therapist.

27. Significant others verbalize an understanding of their role in the process of assisting the client with attaining and maintaining behavioral goals while not enabling client in sexual acting out. (30, 31, 32)

28. Significant others verbally identify their enabling behaviors as well as replacement behaviors that hold client responsible to treatment plan of change. (33)

29. Share with significant other the lies that have been used to hide the sexual compulsions. (34)

30. Verbalize empathy for consequences of sexual acting out on others. (35)

31. Verbalize an awareness of the potential legal consequences of continued sexual acting out. (36)

32. Write a plan for attaining true intimacy in relationship to replace sexual objectification. (37)

33. Commit to long-term recovery plan. (38)

—. _____
   _____
—. _____
   _____
—. _____
   _____

18. Probe client's history for experience of sexual trauma or abuse and assess the effects on current sexual patterns of behavior.

19. Process emotions surrounding an emotional trauma in the sexual arena. (See Sexual Abuse chapter in this *Planner*.)

20. Probe the sense of shame, guilt, and low self-worth that has resulted from sexual acting out.

21. Have client complete a journal describing any struggles and/or successes with sexual behavior plan. Discuss areas that are particularly difficult to maintain with therapist.

22. Inquire about client's progress with maintaining behavior plan. Discuss any relapses with emphasis on possible triggers preceding sexual acting out.

23. Help the client write a plan to cope (e.g., attend a support group meeting, call a sponsor, practice relaxation, utilize spiritual resources, exercise) with each high-risk situation that he/she has identified.

24. Probe client regarding rituals (e.g., cruising neighborhoods, buying pornography) that precede sexual acting out.

25. Assist client in developing a plan of termination of any rituals that precede sexual acting out.

26. Have client list all lies he/she told to hide sexual acting out;

explore with client how this "enabled" the behavior to continue.

27. Have the client list the activities he/she plans to use to increase pleasure while maintaining control over sexual impulses.

28. Using progressive relaxation and deep breathing techniques, teach the client how to relax and suggest that he/she practice this technique daily.

29. Have the client list 10 distraction techniques (e.g., attending a 12-Step meeting, going for a walk, calling a friend/sponsor, taking a bath) to use when experiencing desire for sexual behavior that is outside behavior plan.

30. Ask the client to invite significant others to attend a session.

31. Request the client's significant others attend Codependents of Sex Addicts (C.O.S.A.) or S-Anon meetings.

32. Educate the client's significant other about how denying, minimizing, and excusing client's behavior allows client's sexual acting out to continue to worsen.

33. Assist significant others in identifying their own enabling behaviors that must be terminated and role play or model replacement behaviors that make the client responsible for his/her behavior.

34. Have the client list ways he/she has lied to hide and continue the sexual acting out. Share with partner in session.

35. Ask client to reverse roles with victims/partners of his/her sexual acting out to try to get him/her to develop empathy for the consequences of his/her lack of impulse control.

36. Ask client to accurately and honestly list the potential negative legal consequences of continuing his/her sexual acting out.

37. Ask client to describe his/her ideal intimate relationship and what barriers exist to attaining that ideal; develop a plan to begin to behave in a way that makes attainment of an approximation of that ideal goal possible.

38. Encourage client and his/her significant other to commit to long-term recovery plan. Process any hesitation.

___. _____

_____

___. _____

_____

___. _____

_____

DIAGNOSTIC SUGGESTIONS

Axis I:	302.4	Exhibitionism
	302.81	Fetishism
	302.89	Frotteurism
	302.2	Pedophilia
	302.83	Sexual Masochism
	302.84	Sexual Sadism
	302.82	Voyeurism
	302.9	Paraphilia NOS
	_____	_____
	_____	_____
Axis II:	301.7	Antisocial Personality Disorder
	301.83	Borderline Personality Disorder
	301.81	Narcissistic Personality Disorder
	_____	_____
	_____	_____

SEXUAL IDENTITY CONFUSION—ADOLESCENT

BEHAVIORAL DEFINITIONS

1. Uncertainty about basic sexual orientation.
2. Recent homosexual experimentation which has created questions about sexual orientation.
3. Sexual fantasies, desires, and so on, about same sex partners which cause distress.
4. Recent disclosure of homosexuality to parents.
5. Parents verbalizing distress over concern that child may be homosexual.
6. Parents expressing feelings of failure because child is gay/lesbian.
7. Depressed mood, diminished interest in activities.
8. Feelings of guilt, shame, and/or worthlessness.
9. Concealing sexual identity from parents.

—. _____
   _____
—. _____
   _____
—. _____
   _____

LONG-TERM GOALS

1. Identify sexual identity and engage in a wide range of relationships that are supportive of same.
2. Reduce overall frequency and intensity of the anxiety associated with sexual identity so that daily functioning is not impaired.
3. Disclose sexual orientation to parents.

4. Return to previous level of emotional, psychological, and social functioning.
5. Parents accept child's homosexuality.
6. Resolve all symptoms of depression (e.g., depressed mood, guilt, worthlessness).

—. _____
  _____
  _____
—. _____
  _____
  _____
—. _____
  _____
  _____

SHORT-TERM OBJECTIVES

THERAPEUTIC INTERVENTIONS

1. Describe fear, anxiety, and distress about confusion over sexual identity. (1)

2. Verbalize any suicidal thoughts or impulses. (2)

3. Contract not to harm self. (3)

4. Openly discuss history of sexual desires, fantasies, and experiences. (4)

5. Verbalize reasons for questions about sexual identity. (5)

6. Verbalize an understanding that sexual experimentation with same-sex partners is common and not necessarily an indication of homosexual identity. (6)

7. Rate sexual attraction to males and females on a scale of 1 to 10. (7)

8. Write a "future" biography detailing life as heterosexual and homosexual to assist client

1. Actively build trust with client and encourage his/her expression of fear, anxiety, and distress over sexual identity confusion.

2. Conduct suicide assessment and refer to appropriate level of care if danger to self exists.

3. Encourage client to verbalize and then sign a no-harm contract.

4. Assess client's current sexual functioning by asking about previous sexual history, fantasies, and thoughts.

5. Ask client why he/she has questions about sexuality with specific questions about when he/she began to question sexuality and why.

6. Educate client about the commonality of same-sex experiences in youth and that these

in identifying primary orientation. (8)

9. Identify the negative emotions (e.g., shame, guilt, anxiety, loneliness) experienced by hiding sexuality. (9)

10. Verbalize an understanding of how religious beliefs have contribute to hiding/denying sexual orientation. (10)

11. Verbalize an understanding of safer-sex practices. (11)

12. List ten myths about homosexuals and replace with more realistic, positive beliefs. (12)

13. List advantages and disadvantages of disclosing sexual orientation to significant people in life. (13)

14. Read books that depict lesbian and gay adolescents in positive ways. (14)

15. Watch movies/videos that provide positive role models for lesbian adolescents and depict the family conflict that accompanies disclosure of homosexuality. (15)

16. Describe social interaction with peers and identify any isolation and/or homophobia experienced because of homosexual identity. (16)

17. Attend a support group for gay and lesbian adolescents. (17)

18. Gather support and information from the Internet, web sites, and/or bulletin board services. (18)

do not necessarily indicate a homosexual identity.

7. Have client rate sexual attraction to males and females on a scale of 1 to 10 (with 10 being extremely attracted and 1 being not at all attracted).

8. Assign client homework of writing a "future" biography describing his/her life 20 years in the future, once as a heterosexual another as homosexual. Read and process in session (e.g., ask client which life was more satisfying, which life had more regret).

9. Explore the client's negative emotions related to hiding/denying his/her sexuality.

10. Explore client's religious convictions and how these may conflict with identifying self as homosexual and cause feelings of shame or guilt. (See Religious Conflicts chapter in this *Planner.*)

11. Teach details of safer-sex guidelines.

12. Assign client homework to identify 10 myths about homosexuals (e.g., bad parenting causes homosexuality, homosexuals are not ever happy) and assist in replacing them with more realistic, positive beliefs (e.g., there is no evidence that parenting causes homsexuality, gay men and lesbians are as happy as heterosexuals).

13. Assign client to list advantages and disadvantages of disclosing

19. Identify gay/lesbian youth to socialize with. (19)

20. Write a plan detailing when, where, and to whom sexual orientation is to be disclosed. (20)

21. Role play disclosing sexual orientation to family and other significant people. (21)

22. Reveal sexual orientation to family according to written plan. (22)

23. Verbalize feelings generated by disclosing sexual orientation to family and significant others. (23)

24. Parents attend conjoint sessions that focus on resolving feelings about child's disclosure of homosexual orientation. (24)

25. Parents verbalize their emotional reactions to child's disclosure of homosexuality. (25)

26. Parents verbalize an increased understanding of homosexuality. (26, 27)

27. Parents read books about parenting gay and lesbian offspring. (27)

28. Parents attend a support group. (28)

29. Parents identify any religious beliefs that contribute to rejecting their child's homosexuality. (29)

30. Parents verbalize an understanding that many religious leaders are accepting of homosexuals. (30, 31)

sexual orientation to family and other significant people on life. Process in session.

14. Assign client books which provide accurate, positive messages about homosexual adolescents (e.g., *Reflections of a Rock Lobster* [Fricke], *Not the Only One: Lesbian and Gay Fiction for Teens* [Grima], *Two Teenagers in 20: Writings by Gay and Lesbian Youth* [Heron]).

15. Ask client to watch movies/ videos that depict lesbian and gay adolescents as healthy and happy (e.g., *Incredibly True Adventures of Two Girls in Love, Beautiful Thing,* and *Ma Vie en Rose*). Process reactions in session.

16. Explore client's relationships with peers and assist him/her in describing any homophobic experiences and/or isolation.

17. Refer client to lesbian/gay adolescent support group (e.g., Gay and Lesbian Community Service Center, Youth Services, etc.).

18. Encourage client to gather information and support from the Internet (e.g., The Cool Page for Queer Teens, The Internet news group soc.support.youth. gay-lesbian-bi).

19. Encourage client to identify other lesbian and gay adolescents to interact with by reviewing people he/she has met in support groups, at work, and

___. _____
_____

___. _____
_____

___. _____
_____

so on, and encourage him/her to initiate social activities.

20. Assign client homework to write a detailed plan to disclose sexual orientation, including to whom it will be disclosed, where, when, and possible questions and reactions recipient might have.

21. Have client role play disclosure of sexual orientation to significant others.

22. Encourage client to disclose sexual orientation to family according to previously written plan.

23. Probe client about reactions of significant others to disclosure of homosexuality. Provide encouragement and positive feedback.

24. Arrange conjoint sessions and encourage parents to attend and participate.

25. Explore emotional reactions of parents to disclosure of child's homosexuality.

26. Educate parents about homosexuality and answer questions they have in honest, direct manner (e.g., assure parents that homosexuality is not caused by faulty parenting or considered a mental illness).

27. Assign parents books that offer positive realistic information about homosexuality and homosexual adolescents (e.g., *Is It a Choice?* [Marcus], *Beyond Acceptance: Parents of*

Lesbians and Gays Talk About Their Experiences [Griffin, Wirth, & Wirth]).

28. Refer parents to a support group (e.g., Parents and Friends of Lesbians and Gays) and encourage their attendance.

29. Probe parents about religious beliefs regarding homosexuality.

30. Refer parents to gay/lesbian positive clergy to discuss their concerns.

31. Assign parents to read Chapter Four of *Beyond Acceptance* (Griffin, Wirth, & Wirth). Process reactions in session.

___. _____

_____

___. _____

_____

___. _____

_____

DIAGNOSTIC SUGGESTIONS

Axis I:	309.0	Adjustment Disorder with Depressed Mood
	309.28	Adjustment Disorder with Mixed Anxiety and Depressed Mood
	300.00	Anxiety Disorder NOS
	309.24	Adjustment Disorder with Anxiety
	300.4	Dysthymic Disorder
	302.85	Gender Identity Disorder in Adolescents or Adults
	300.02	Generalized Anxiety Disorder
	313.82	Identity Problem
	296.2x	Major Depressive Disorder, Single Episode
	296.3x	Major Depressive Disorder, Recurrent
	V62.89	Phase of Life Problem
	V61.20	Parent-Child Relational Problem
	302.9	Sexual Disorder Not Otherwise Specified
	_____	_____
	_____	_____

SEXUAL IDENTITY CONFUSION—ADULT

BEHAVIORAL DEFINITIONS

1. Uncertainty about basic sexual orientation.
2. Difficulty enjoying sexual activities with opposite sex partner because of low arousal.
3. Sexual fantasies, desires, and so on, about same sex partners which cause distress.
4. Engagement in sexual activity with person of same sex which has caused confusion, guilt, and anxiety.
5. Depressed mood, diminished interest in activities.
6. Marital conflicts caused by uncertainty about sexual orientation.
7. Feelings of guilt, shame, and/or worthlessness.
8. Concealing sexual identity from significant others (e.g., friends, family, spouse).

__. _____
    _____
__. _____
    _____
__. _____
    _____

LONG-TERM GOALS

1. Identify sexual identity and engage in a wide range of relationships that are supportive of same.
2. Reduce overall frequency and intensity of the anxiety associated with sexual identity so that daily functioning is not impaired.
3. Disclose sexual orientation to important people in client's life.

4. Return to previous level of emotional, psychological, and social functioning.
5. Eliminate all signs of depression (e.g., depressed mood, guilt, worthlessness).

—. _____

—. _____

—. _____

SHORT-TERM OBJECTIVES

1. Describe fear, anxiety, and distress about confusion over sexual identity. (1)

2. Openly discuss history of sexual desires, fantasies, and experiences with therapist. (2)

3. Identify sexual experiences that have been source of excitement, satisfaction, and emotional gratification. (3)

4. Write a journal describing sexual thoughts, fantasies and conflicts that occur throughout the week and discuss in session with therapist. (4)

5. Rate sexual attraction to men and women on a scale of 1 to 10. (5)

6. Verbalize an understanding of how cultural, racial, and/or ethnic identity contributes to confusion about sexual identity. (6)

7. Write a "future" biography detailing life as heterosexual

THERAPEUTIC INTERVENTIONS

1. Actively build trust with client and encourage his/her expression of fear, anxiety and distress over sexual identity confusion.

2. Assess client's current sexual functioning by asking about previous sexual history, fantasies, and thoughts.

3. Assist client in identifying sexual experiences that have been source of excitement, satisfaction, and emotional gratification.

4. Assign client to write a journal describing sexual thoughts, fantasies, and conflicts that occur throughout the week to assist him/her in increasing awareness of sexual attractions and conflicts.

5. Have client rate sexual attraction to men and women on a scale of 1 to 10 (with 10 being extremely attracted and 1 being not at all attracted).

and homosexual to assist client in identifying primary orientation. (7)

8. Verbalize an understanding of the range of sexual identities possible. (8, 9)

9. Identify the negative emotions (e.g., shame, guilt, anxiety, loneliness) experienced by hiding sexuality. (10)

10. Verbalize an understanding of how religious beliefs have contributed to hiding/denying sexual orientation. (11)

11. Verbalize an understanding of safer-sex practices. (12)

12. List ten myths about homosexuals and replace with more realistic, positive beliefs. (13)

13. Verbalize an increased understanding of homosexuality. (8, 13, 15)

14. List advantages and disadvantages of disclosing sexual orientation to significant people in life. (14)

15. Read books on disclosing sexual orientation to significant others. (15)

16. Watch films/videos that depict lesbian women/gay men in positive ways. (16)

17. Attend a support group for those who want to disclose themselves as homosexual. (17)

18. Read local gay/lesbian newspapers, magazines, and/or Yellow Pages to identify social activities for gay men or lesbians. (18)

6. Explore with client how cultural, ethnic, and/or racial group defines and views homosexual behavior and/or identity.

7. Assign client homework of writing a "future" biography describing his/her life 20 years in the future, once as a heterosexual, another as homosexual. Read and process in session (e.g., ask client which life was more satisfying, which life had more regret).

8. Educate client about the range of sexual identities possible (e.g., heterosexual, homosexual, bisexual).

9. Have client read *The Invention of Heterosexuality* (Katz).

10. Explore the client's negative emotions related to hiding/denying her/his sexuality.

11. Explore client's religious convictions and how these may conflict with identifying self as homosexual and cause feelings of shame or guilt. (See Religious Conflicts chapter in this *Planner*.)

12. Teach details of safer-sex guidelines and encourage client to include them in all future sexual activity.

13. Assign client homework to identify 10 myths about homosexuals and assist in replacing them with more realistic, positive beliefs.

14. Assign client to list advantages and disadvantages of disclosing

19. Gather support and information from the Internet, web sites, and/or bulletin board services. (19)

20. Identify gay/lesbian people to socialize with. (20)

21. Role play disclosing sexual orientation to significant others (e.g., family, friends, coworkers). (21)

22. Write a plan detailing when, where, and to whom sexual orientation is to be disclosed. (22)

23. Identify one friend who is likely to have positive reaction to client disclosing homosexuality. (23, 24)

24. Reveal sexual orientation to significant others according to written plan. (25)

25. Explore results (e.g, acceptance, rejection, shock) of disclosing sexual orientation. (26)

___. _____
   _____
___. _____
   _____
___. _____
   _____

sexual orientation to significant others. Process in session.

15. Assign client books which provide accurate, positive messages about homosexuality (e.g., *Is it a Choice?* [Marcus], *Outing Yourself* [Signorile], or *Coming Out: An Act of Love* [Eichberg]).

16. Ask client to watch movies/videos that depict lesbians/gay men as healthy and happy (e.g., *Desert Hearts, In and Out, Jeffrey,* and *When Night Is Falling*). Process reactions in session.

17. Refer client to coming out support group at Gay and Lesbian Community Service Center, AIDS Project, and so on.

18. Assign client to read lesbian/gay magazines and newspapers (e.g, *The Advocate*).

19. Encourage client to gather information and support from the Internet (e.g., coming out bulletin boards on AOL, lesbian/gay organizations' web sites).

20. Encourage client to identify gay men or lesbians to interact with by reviewing people he/she has met in support groups, at work, and so on, and encourage him/her to initiate social activities.

21. Have client role play disclosure of sexual orientation to significant others. (See Family of Origin Conflicts chapter in this *Planner.*)

22. Assign client homework to write a detailed plan to disclose sexual orientation, including to whom it will be disclosed, where, when, and possible questions and reactions recipient(s) might have.

23. Encourage client to identify one friend who is likely to be accepting of her/his homosexuality.

24. Suggest client have casual talks about lesbian/gay rights, or some item in the news related to lesbians and gay men to "test the water" before disclosing sexual orientation to friend.

25. Encourage client to disclose sexual orientation to friend/family according to plan.

26. Probe client about reactions of significant others to disclosure of homosexuality. Provide encouragement and positive feedback.

——. _____

_____

——. _____

_____

——. _____

_____

DIAGNOSTIC SUGGESTIONS

Axis I:	309.0	Adjustment Disorder with Depressed Mood
	309.28	Adjustment Disorder with Mixed Anxiety and Depressed Mood
	300.00	Anxiety Disorder NOS
	309.24	Adjustment Disorder with Anxiety
	300.4	Dysthymic Disorder
	302.85	Gender Identity Disorder in Adolescents or Adults
	300.02	Generalized Anxiety Disorder
	313.82	Identity Problem
	296.2x	Major Depressive Disorder, Single Episode
	296.3x	Major Depressive Disorder, Recurrent
	V62.89	Phase of Life Problem
	V61.20	Parent-Child Relational Problem
	302.9	Sexual Disorder Not Otherwise Specified
	_____	_____
	_____	_____
Axis II:	301.82	Avoidant Personality Disorder
	301.83	Borderline Personality Disorder
	301.81	Narcissistic Personality Disorder
	_____	_____
	_____	_____

Appendix A

BIBLIOTHERAPY SUGGESTIONS

ADOPTION/SURROGACY

Benkov, L. (1994). *Reinventing the Family: Lesbian and Gay Relationships That Last.* New York: Crown Publishing Group.

Clunis, D., & Green, G. (1995). *The Lesbian Parenting Book: A Guide to Creating Families and Raising Children.* Seattle: Seal Press.

Folberg, J. (1991). *Joint Custody and Shared Parenting.* New York: Guilford Press.

Gil de Lamadrid, M. (1991). *Lesbians Choosing Motherhood: Legal Implications of Donor Insemination and Co-parenting.* San Francisco: National Center for Lesbian Rights.

Lancaster, K. (1996). *Keys to Parenting an Adopted Child.* New York: Barron's Publishers.

Martin, A. (1993). *The Lesbian and Gay Parenting Handbook: Creating and Raising Our Families.* New York: HarperCollins.

Morgen, K. (1995). *Getting Simon: Two Gay Doctors' Journey to Fatherhood.* Bearsville: Bramble Books.

AGING

Adelman, M. (1986). *Long Time Passing: Lives of Older Lesbians.* Boston: Alyson.

Berger, R. (1996). *Gay and Gray: The Older Homosexual Man.* New York: Haworth Press.

Signorile, M. (1997). *Life Outside: The Signorile Report on Gay Men: Sex, Drugs, Muscles, and the Passages of Life.* New York: HarperPerennial.

ANXIETY

Beck, A., Emery, G., & Greenberg, R. (1990). *Anxiety Disorders and Phobias: A Cognitive Perspective.* New York: Basic Books.

Burns, D. (1989). *The Feeling Good Handbook.* New York: Plume.

Burns, D. (1993). *Ten Days to Self-Esteem!* New York: William Morrow.

Davis, M., Robbins-Eshelman, E., McKay, M., & Eshelman, B. (1998). *Relaxation and Stress Reduction Workbook.* New York: Harbinger.

Haley, J. (1994). *Ordeal Therapy.* New York: Jossey Bass.

BREAST CANCER

Burns, D. (1993). *Ten Days to Self-Esteem!* New York: William Morrow.

Butler, S., & Rosenblaum, B. (1991). *Cancer in Two Voices.* Duluth, MN: Spinsters Ink.

Love, S. (1995). *Dr. Susan Love's Breast Book.* New York: Perseus Press.

White, J., & Martinez, C. (1997). *The Lesbian Health Book.* Seattle: Seal Press.

CHEMICAL DEPENDENCE

Crawford, D. (1990). *Easing the Ache: Gay Men Recovering from Compulsive Behaviors.* New York: Dutton.

Isensee, R. (1991). *Growing Up Gay in a Dysfunctional Family: A Guide for Gay Men Reclaiming Their Lives.* New York: Simon & Schuster.

DEPRESSION

Burns, D. (1989). *The Feeling Good Handbook.* New York: Plume.

Butler, P. (1991). *Talking to Yourself: Learning the Language of Self-Affirmation.* New York: Stein and Day.

Hallinan, P.K. (1976). *One Day at a Time.* Minneapolis, MN: CompCare.

Hazelden Staff. (1991). *Each Day a New Beginning.* Center City, MN: Hazelden.

Helmstetter, S. (1990). *What to Say When You Talk to Yourself.* New York: Pocket Books.

Isensee, R. (1991). *Growing Up Gay in a Dysfunctional Family: A Guide for Gay Men Reclaiming Their Lives.* New York: Simon & Schuster.

EMPLOYMENT DISCRIMINATION

Baker, D., O'Brien, S., & Henning, B. (1995). *Cracking the Corporate Closet: The 200 Best (and Worst) Companies to Work for, Buy from, and Invest in if You're Gay and Lesbian—and Even if You Aren't.* New York: Harper-Business.

Friskopp, A., & Silverstein, S. (1995). *Straight Companies, Gay Lives: Gay and Lesbian Professionals, The Harvard Business School and the American Workplace.* New York: Simon & Schuster.

McNaught, B. (1993). *Gay Issues in the Workplace.* New York: St. Martin's Press.

Rasi, R., & Rodriguez-Nogues, L. (1999). *Out in the Workplace: Gay and Lesbian Professionals Tell Their Stories.* Boston: Alyson Publications.

FAMILY OF ORIGIN CONFLICTS

Borhek, M. (1979). *My Son Eric.* New York: Pilgrim Press.

Borhek, M. (1993). *Coming Out to Parents: A Two-Way Survival Guide for Lesbians and Gay Men and Their Parents.* New York: Pilgrim Press.

Clark, D. (1997). *Loving Someone Gay.* Berkeley: Celestial Arts Publishing.

Cohen, S., & Cohen, D. (1992). *When Someone You Know Is Gay.* New York: Laurel-Leaf Books.

Dew, D. (1993). *The Family Heart: A Memoir of When Our Son Came Out.* New York: HarperCollins.

Fairchild, B., & Hayward, N. (1989). *Now That You Know: What Every Parent Should Know About Homosexuality.* San Diego: Harcourt Brace Jovanovich.

Griffin, C., Wirth, A., & Wirth, M. (1996). *Beyond Acceptance: Parents of Lesbian and Gays Talk about Their Experiences.* New York: St. Martin's Press.

Isensee, R. (1991). *Growing Up Gay in a Dysfunctional Family: A Guide for Gay Men Reclaiming Their Lives.* New York: Simon & Schuster.

Marcus, E. (1993). *Is It a Choice? Answers to 300 of the Most Frequently Asked Questions About Gays and Lesbians.* San Francisco: Harper.

Signorile, M. (1996). *Outing Yourself: How to Come Out as Lesbian or Gay to Your Family, Friends and Coworkers.* New York: Fireside Books.

FEMALE SEXUAL DYSFUNCTION

Barbach, L., & Levine, L. (1990). *Shared Intimacies: Women's Sexual Experiences.* New York: Doubleday.

Boston Women's Health Collective. (1985). *The New Our Bodies, Our Selves.* Boston: Simon & Schuster.

Caster, W. (1993). *The Lesbian Sex Book.* Boston: Alyson Publications.

Loulan, J. (1984). *Lesbian Sex.* Duluth, MN: Spinsters Ink.

Wolf, N. (1992). *The Beauty Myth: How Images of Beauty Are Used Against Women.* Anchor.

GRIEF MULTIPLE LOSS

Kubler-Ross, E. (1997). *AIDS: The Ultimate Challenge.* Collier Books.

Monette, P. (1988). *Borrowed Time: An AIDS Memoir.* New York: Harcourt Brace.

Odets, W. (1995). *In the Shadow of the Epidemic: Being HIV Negative in the Age of AIDS.* Durham, NC: Duke University Press.

Shernoff, M., & Picano, F. (1998). *Gay Widowers: Life After the Death of a Partner.* New York: Haworth Press.

HATE CRIMES VICTIM

Herek, G. (1991). *Hate Crimes: Confronting Violence Against Lesbians and Gay Men.* Los Angeles: Sage.

HIV/AIDS

Burns, D. (1993). *Ten Days to Self-Esteem!* New York: William Morrow.

Cousins, N. (1991). *Anatomy of an Illness.* New York: Doubleday.

Kalichman, S. (1998). *Understanding AIDS: Advances in Research and Treatment.* Washington, DC: American Psychological Association.

Kubler-Ross, E. (1997). *AIDS: The Ultimate Challenge.* Collier Books.

LeShan, L. (1977). *You Can Fight for Your Life.* New York: M. Evans & Co.

Monette, P. (1988). *Borrowed Time: An AIDS Memoir.* New York: Harcourt Brace.

Shernoff, M., & Picano, F. (1998). *Gay Widowers: Life After the Death of a Partner.* New York: Haworth Press.

HIV NEGATIVE/HIV POSITIVE COUPLE

Berzon, B. (1996). *The Intimacy Dance: A Guide to Long Term Success in Gay and Lesbian Relationships.* New York: Penguin Books.

Berzon, B. (1998). *Permanent Partners: Building Gay and Lesbian Relationships That Last.* New York: E.P. Dutton.

Isensee, R. (1990). *Love Between Men: Enhancing Intimacy and Keeping Your Relationship Alive.* Los Angeles: Alyson Publications.

Odets, W. (1995). *In the Shadow of the Epidemic: Being HIV Negative in the Age of AIDS.* Durham, NC: Duke University Press.

HOMOSEXUAL MARRIED TO HETEROSEXUAL

Buxton, A. (1994). *The Other Side of the Closet: The Coming-Out Crisis for Straight Spouses and Families.* New York: Wiley Publishers.

Heron, A., & Maran, M. (1991). *How Would You Feel If Your Dad Was Gay?* Boston: Alyson Publications.

Miller, D. (1993). *Coping When a Parent Is Gay.* New York: Rosen Publishing Group.

INTERNALIZED HOMOPHOBIA

Blumenfeld, W. (1992). *Homophobia: The Price We All Pay.* Boston: Beacon.

Sears, J., & Williams, W. (1997). *Overcoming Heterosexism and Homophobia: Strategies That Work.* New York: Columbia University Press.

INTIMATE RELATIONSHIP CONFLICTS

Berzon, B. (1996). *The Intimacy Dance: A Guide to Long Term Success in Gay and Lesbian Relationships.* New York: Penguin Books.

Berzon, B. (1998). *Permanent Partners: Building Gay and Lesbian Relationships That Last.* New York: E.P. Dutton.

Blumstein, P., & Schwartz, P. (1983). *American Couples: Money, Work, Sex.* New York: William Morrow.

Boston Lesbian Psychologies Collective. (Eds.). (1987). *Lesbian Psychologies.* Chicago: University of Illinois Press.

Clunis, D., & Green, G. (1988). *Lesbian Couples.* Seattle: Seal Press.

Colgrove, B., Bloomfield, D., & McWilliams, C. (1997). *How to Survive the Loss of a Love.* New York: Dolphin Books.

Driggs, J., & Finn, S. (1991). *Intimacy Between Men: How to Find and Keep Gay Love Relationships.* New York: Penguin Books.

Hall, M. (1989). *The Lesbian Love Companion: How to Survive Everything from Heartthrob to Heartbreak.* New York: HarperCollins.

Hendricks, D. (1989). *Getting the Love You Want.* New York: HarperCollins.

Isensee, R. (1990). *Love Between Men: Enhancing Intimacy and Keeping Your Relationship Alive.* Los Angeles: Alyson Publications.

Johnson, S. (1990). *Staying Power: Long Term Lesbian Couples.* New York: Naiad Press.

Martinac, P. (1998). *The Lesbian and Gay Book of Love and Marriage.* New York: Broadway Books.

LEGAL CONFLICTS

Curry, H., Clifford, D., & Leonard, R. (1996). *A Legal Guide for Lesbian and Gay Couples*. Berkeley, CA: Nolo Press, Inc.

MALE SEXUAL DYSFUNCTION

Hart, J. (1998). *Gay Sex: A Manual for Men Who Love Men*. Los Angeles: Alyson Publications.

Isensee, R. (1990). *Love Between Men: Enhancing Intimacy and Keeping Your Relationship Alive*. Los Angeles: Alyson Publications.

Palermo, T. (1997). *Sex Advisor: The 100 Most Asked Questions About Sex Between Men*. Los Angeles: Alyson Press.

Silverstein, C., & Picano, F. (1992). *The New Joy of Gay Sex*. New York: HarperPerennial.

PARENTING CONFLICTS

Barret, R., & Robinson, B. (1990). *Gay Fathers*. Lexington: Lexington Books.

Benkov, L. (1994). *Reinventing the Family: Lesbian and Gay Parents*. New York: Crown Publishing Group.

Bosche, S. (1981). *Jenny Lives with Eric and Martin*. London: Gay Men's Press.

Briggs, D. (1975). *Your Child's Self Esteem: Step by Step Guidelines for Raising Responsible, Productive, Happy Children*. New York: Dolphin Books.

Casper, V., & Schultz, S. (1999). *Gay Parents/Straight Schools: Building Communication and Trust*. New York: Teachers College Press.

Clunis, D., & Green, G. (1995). *The Lesbian Parenting Book: A Guide to Creating Families and Raising Children*. Seattle: Seal Press.

Corley, R. (1990). *The Final Closet: A Gay Parent's Guide for Coming Out to Their Children*. Miami: Editech Press.

Dinkmeyer, D., & McKay, G. (1982). *The Parent's Handbook: Systematic Training for Effective Parenting*. Circle Pines: American Guidance Service, Inc.

Folberg, J. (1991). *Joint Custody and Shared Parenting*. New York: Guilford Press.

Heron, A., & Maran, M. (1991). *How Would You Feel If Your Dad Was Gay?* Boston: Alyson Publications.

Lancaster, K. (1996). *Keys to Parenting an Adopted Child*. New York: Barron's Publishers.

Martin, A. (1993). *The Lesbian and Gay Parenting Handbook: Creating and Raising Our Families*. New York: HarperCollins.

McCarney, S., & Bauer, A. (1990). *The Parent's Guide: Solutions to Today's Most Common Behavior Problems in the Home.* Columbia: Hawthorne Educational Services, Inc.

Miller, D. (1993). *Coping When a Parent Is Gay.* New York: Rosen Publishing Group.

Newman, L. (1989). *Heather Has Two Mommies.* Boston: Alyson Publications.

Newman, L. (1991). *Gloria Goes to Gay Pride.* Boston: Alyson Wonderland.

Pollack, J. (1995). *Lesbian and Gay Families: Redefining Parenting in America.* New York: Franklin Watts.

Severance, J. (1983). *Lots of Mommies.* Chapel Hill, NC: Lollipop Power.

Valentine, J. (1993). *Two Moms, the Zark, and Me.* Boston: Alyson Wonderland.

Valentine, J. (1994). *One Dad, Two Dads, Brown Dads, Blue Dads.* Boston: Alyson Wonderland.

Willhoite, M. (1990). *Daddy's Roommate.* Boston: Alyson Publications.

PHYSICAL ABUSE VICTIM

Island, D., & Letellier, P. (1991). *Men Who Beat the Men Who Love Them.* New York: Harrington Park Press.

Lobell, K. (1986). *Naming the Violence: Speaking Out about Lesbian Battering.* Seattle: Seal Press.

RELIGIOUS CONFLICTS

Boswell, J. (1989). *Christianity, Social Tolerance and Homosexuality: Gay People in Western Europe from the Beginning of the Christian Era to the Fourteenth Century.* Chicago: University of Chicago Press.

McNeill, J. (1995). *Freedom, Glorious Freedom: The Spiritual Journey to the Fullness of Life for Gays, Lesbians and Everybody Else.* Boston: Beacon Press.

White, M. (1995). *Stranger at the Gate: To Be Gay and Christian in America.* New York: Plume.

Winterson, J. (1985). *Oranges Are Not the Only Fruit.* New York: Atlantic Monthly Press.

SAFER SEX

Hart, J. (1998). *Gay Sex: A Manual for Men Who Love Men.* Los Angeles: Alyson Publications.

Odets, W. (1995). *In the Shadow of the Epidemic: Being HIV Negative in the Age of AIDS.* Durham, NC: Duke University Press.

Palermo, T. (1998). *Sex Adviser: The 100 Most Asked Questions About Sex Between Men.* Boston: Alyson Publications.

Silverstein, C., & Picano, F. (1992). *The New Joy of Gay Sex.* New York: HarperPerennial.

SEPARATION

Berzon, B. (1996). *The Intimacy Dance: A Guide to Long Term Success in Gay and Lesbian Relationships.* New York: Penguin Books.

Berzon, B. (1998). *Permanent Partners: Building Gay and Lesbian Relationships That Last.* New York: E.P. Dutton.

Clunis, D., & Green, G. (1988). *Lesbian Couples.* Seattle: Seal Press.

Colgrove, B., Bloomfield, D., & McWilliams, C. (1997). *How to Survive the Loss of a Love.* New York: Dolphin Books.

Hall, M. (1989). *The Lesbian Love Companion: How to Survive Everything from Heartthrob to Heartbreak.* New York: HarperCollins.

Martinac, P. (1998). *The Lesbian and Gay Book of Love and Marriage.* New York: Broadway Books.

SEXUAL ABUSE

Bass, E., & Davis, L. (1994). *The Courage to Heal: A Guide for Women Survivors of Child Sexual Abuse.* New York: HarperPerennial Library.

Lew, M. (1990). *Victims No Longer: Men Recovering from Incest and Other Sexual Abuse.* New York: HarperCollins.

SEXUAL ACTING OUT

Carnes, P. (1983). *Out of the Shadows: Understanding Sexual Addiction.* Minneapolis, MN: Compcare.

SEXUAL IDENTITY CONFUSION—ADOLESCENT

Fricke, A. (1995). *Reflections of a Rock Lobster.* New York: Consortium.

Griffin, C., Wirth, A., & Wirth M. (1996). *Beyond Acceptance: Parents of Lesbian and Gays Talk about Their Experiences.* New York: St Martin's Press.

Grima, T. (Ed.). (1995). *Not the Only One: Lesbian and Gay Fiction for Teens.* Boston: Alyson.

Heron, A. (Ed.). (1995). *Two Teenagers in 20: Writings by Gay and Lesbian Youth.* Boston: Alyson.

Jennings, K. (Ed.). (1994). *Becoming Visible: A Reader in Gay and Lesbian History for High School and College Students.* Los Angeles: Alyson.

Marcus, E. (1993). *Is It a Choice? Answers to 300 of the Most Frequently Asked Questions About Gays and Lesbians.* San Francisco: Harper.

SEXUAL IDENTITY CONFUSION—ADULT

Beam, J. (1986). *In the Life: A Black Gay Anthology.* Boston: Alyson Publications.

Eichberg, R. (1991). *Coming Out: An Act of Love.* New York: Penguin.

Katz, J. (1996). *The Invention of Heterosexuality.* New York: Plume.

Marcus, E. (1993). *Is It a Choice? Answers to 300 of the Most Frequently Asked Questions About Gays and Lesbians.* San Francisco: Harper.

Signorile, M. (1996). *Outing Yourself: How to Come Out as Lesbian or Gay to Your Family, Friends, and Coworkers.* New York: Fireside Books.

Appendix B

INDEX OF *DSM-IV* CODES ASSOCIATED WITH PRESENTING PROBLEMS

Acute Stress Disorder 308.30
  Hate Crime Victim
  Physical Abuse Victim
  Sexual Abuse

Adjustment Disorder with Anxiety 309.24
  Adoption/Surrogacy
  Aging
  Anxiety
  Breast Cancer
  Employment Discrimination
  Family of Origin Conflicts
  Hate Crime Victim
  Homosexual Married to
  Heterosexual
  HIV/AIDS
  HIV Negative/HIV Positive
  Couple
  Internalized Homophobia
  Intimate Relationship Conflicts
  Legal Conflicts
  Parenting Conflicts
  Physical Abuse Victim
  Religious Conflicts
  Safer Sex
  Separation
  Sexual Identity Confusion—
  Adolescent
  Sexual Identity Confusion—
  Adult

Adjustment Disorder with Depressed Mood 309.00
  Adoption/Surrogacy
  Aging
  Breast Cancer
  Depression
  Employment Discrimination
  Family of Origin Conflicts
  Grief/Multiple Loss
  Hate Crime Victim
  Homosexual Married to
  Heterosexual
  HIV/AIDS
  HIV Negative/HIV Positive
  Couple
  Internalized Homophobia
  Intimate Relationship Conflicts
  Legal Conflicts
  Parenting Conflicts
  Physical Abuse Victim
  Religious Conflicts
  Safer Sex
  Separation
  Sexual Identity Confusion—
  Adolescent
  Sexual Identity Confusion—Adult

Adjustment Disorders with Disturbance of Conduct 309.30
  Grief/Multiple Loss
  Parenting Conflicts

Adjustment Disorder with Mixed Anxiety and Depressed Mood   309.28

Adoption/Surrogacy
Aging
Breast Cancer
Family of Origin Conflicts
Hate Crime Victim
Homosexual Married to
Heterosexual
HIV/AIDS
HIV Negative/HIV Positive
Couple
Internalized Homophobia
Intimate Relationship Conflicts
Legal Conflicts
Parenting Conflicts
Physical Abuse Victim
Religious Conflicts
Safer Sex
Separation
Sexual Identity Confusion—
Adolescent
Sexual Identity Confusion—Adult

Adjustment Disorder with Mixed Disturbance of Emotions and Conduct   309.40

Homosexual Married to
Heterosexual
Legal Conflicts
Parenting Conflicts
Separation

Alcohol Abuse   305.00

Chemical Dependence
Legal Conflicts
Physical Abuse Victim

Alcohol Dependence   303.90

Chemical Dependence
Physical Abuse Victim

Amphetamine Abuse   305.70

Chemical Dependence
Legal Conflicts

Amphetamine Dependence   304.40

Chemical Dependence

Antisocial Personality Disorder   301.70

Chemical Dependence
Legal Conflicts
Safer Sex
Sexual Acting Out

Anxiety Disorder NOS   300.00

Aging
Anxiety
Employment Discrimination
Family of Origin Conflicts
Homosexual Married to
Heterosexual
Sexual Identity Confusion—
Adolescent
Sexual Identity Confusion—Adult

Avoidant Personality Disorder   301.82

Intimate Relationship Conflicts
Sexual Abuse
Sexual Identity Confusion—Adult

Bereavement   V62.82

Aging
Depression
Grief/Multiple Loss

Bipolar I Disorder   296.xx

Depression

Bipolar II Disorder   296.89

Depression

Body Dysmorphic Disorder   300.70

Male Sexual Dysfunction

Borderline Personality Disorder   301.83

Chemical Dependence
Hate Crime Victim
Physical Abuse Victim
Safer Sex
Separation
Sexual Abuse
Sexual Acting Out
Sexual Identity Confusion—Adult

Cannabis Abuse 305.20
Chemical Dependence
Legal Conflicts

Cannabis Dependence 304.30
Chemical Dependence

Cocaine Abuse 305.60
Chemical Dependence
Legal Conflicts

Cocaine Dependence 304.20
Chemical Dependence

Cyclothymic Disorder 301.13
Depression

**Dementia Due to Parkinson's
Disease** 294.10
Aging

**Dementia Due to HIV Disease
294.90**
Aging

**Dementia Due to
Creutzfeldt-Jakob Disease** 290.10
Aging

**Dementia Due to ...
[Indicate the General
Medical Condition]** 294.10
Aging
HIV/AIDS

**Dependent Personality
Disorder** 301.60
Hate Crime Victim
Intimate Relationship Conflicts
Physical Abuse Victim
Separation
Sexual Abuse

Depressive Disorder NOS 311
Homosexual Married to
Heterosexual

Dissociative Amnesia 300.12
Hate Crime Victim
Sexual Abuse

Dissociative Disorder NOS 300.15
Sexual Abuse

**Dissociative Identity
Disorder** 300.14
Sexual Abuse

**Dyspareunia (Not Due
to a General Medical
Condition)** 302.76
Female Sexual Dysfunction
Male Sexual Dysfunction

Dysthymic Disorder 300.40
Aging
Breast Cancer
Depression
Employment Discrimination
Family of Origin Conflicts
Grief/Multiple Loss
Hate Crime Victim
Homosexual Married to
Heterosexual
HIV/AIDS
HIV Negative/HIV Positive
Couple
Internalized Homophobia
Male Sexual Dysfunction
Parenting Conflicts
Physical Abuse Victim
Religious Conflicts
Safer Sex
Separation
Sexual Abuse
Sexual Identity Confusion—
Adolescent
Sexual Identity Confusion—Adult

Exhibitionism 302.40
Sexual Acting Out

**Female Dyspareunia Due
to ... [Indicate the General
Medical Condition]** 625.00
Female Sexual Dysfunction

**Female Hypoactive Sexual
Desire Disorder Due
to ... [Indicate the
General Medical Condition]** 625.80
Female Sexual Dysfunction

HIV/AIDS
Parenting Conflicts
Safer Sex
Sexual Identity Confusion—
Adolescent
Sexual Identity Confusion—Adult

Maladaptive Health Behaviors Affecting ... [Indicate the General Medical Condition]   316.00
Breast Cancer
HIV/AIDS
Safer Sex

Male Dyspareunia Due to ... [Indicate the General Medical Condition]   608.89
Male Sexual Dysfunction

Male Erectile Disorder   302.72
Male Sexual Dysfunction

Male Erectile Disorder Due to ... [Indicate the General Medical Condition]   607.84
Male Sexual Dysfunction

Male Hypoactive Sexual Desire Disorder Due to ... [Indicate the General Medical Condition]   608.89
Male Sexual Dysfunction

Male Orgasmic Disorder   302.74
Male Sexual Dysfunction

Mood Disorder Due to ... [Indicate the General Medical Condition]   293.83
HIV Negative/HIV Positive Couple

Narcissistic Personality Disorder   301.81
Aging
Chemical Dependence
Internalized Homophobia
Intimate Relationship Conflicts
Legal Conflicts
Safer Sex
Separation

Sexual Acting Out
Sexual Identity Confusion—Adult

Noncompliance with Treatment   V15.81
Breast Cancer
HIV/AIDS

Occupational Problem   V62.20
Employment Discrimination

Opioid Abuse   305.50
Chemical Dependence

Opioid Dependence   304.00
Chemical Dependence

Paraphilia NOS   302.90
Sexual Acting Out

Parent-Child Relational Problem   V61.20
Family of Origin Conflicts
Homosexual Married to Heterosexual
Parenting Conflicts
Sexual Identity Confusion—
Adolescent
Sexual Identity Confusion—Adult

Partner Relational Problem   V61.10
Adoption/Surrogacy
Female Sexual Dysfunction
Homosexual Married to Heterosexual
HIV Negative/HIV Positive Couple
Internalized Homophobia
Intimate Relationship Conflicts
Male Sexual Dysfunction
Physical Abuse Victim
Separation

Partner Relational Problem NOS   V62.81
Adoption/Surrogacy

Pedophilia   302.20
Sexual Acting Out

TheraScribe® 3.5 for Windows®
The Computerized Assistant to Psychotherapy Treatment Planning

➜ Used in thousands of behavioral health practices and treatment facilities, *TheraScribe® 3.5* is a state-of-the-art *Windows®*-based treatment planning program which rapidly generates comprehensive treatment plans meeting the requirements of all major accrediting agencies and most third-party payers.

➜ In just minutes, this user-friendly program enables you to create customized treatment plans by choosing from thousands of prewritten built-in short-term goals, long-term objectives, therapeutic interventions, automated progress notes, and much more.

➜ This networkable software also tracks treatment outcome, stores clinical pathways, and provides ample room for narrative patient histories, treatment summaries, and discharge notes.

➜ And best of all, this flexible system can be expanded to include the data in this *Gay & Lesbian Psychotherapy Treatment Planner.*

✆GAY & LESBIAN PSYCHOTHERAPY Upgrade to THERASCRIBE 3.5✆

The behavioral definitions, goals, objectives, and interventions from this *Gay & Lesbian Psychotherapy Treatment Planner* can be imported into *TheraScribe® 3.5: The Computerized Assistant to Treatment Planning.* For purchase and pricing information, please send in the coupon below.

- -

For more information about **TheraScribe® 3.5** or the **Gay & Lesbian Psychotherapy Upgrade,** fill in this coupon, and mail it to: M. Fellin, John Wiley & Sons, Inc., 605 Third Avenue, New York, NY 10158

❑ Please send me information on *TheraScribe® 3.5*
❑ Please send me information on the *Gay & Lesbian Psychotherapy Upgrade to TheraScribe® 3.5*

Name _____

Affiliation _____

Address _____

City/State/Zip _____

Phone _____

WILEY
Publishers Since 1807

Practice Planners™ offer mental health professionals a full array of practice management tools. These easy-to-use resources include *Treatment Planners*, which cover all the necessary elements for developing formal treatment plans, including detailed problem definitions, long-term goals, short-term objectives, therapeutic interventions, and DSM-IV diagnoses; *Homework Planners* featuring behaviorally-based, ready-to-use assignments which are designed for use between sessions; and *Documentation Sourcebooks* that provide all the forms and records that therapists need to run their practice.

Practice *Planners*™

WILEY
Publishers Since 1807

ABOUT THE DISK*

TheraScribe® 3.0 and 3.5 Library Module Installation

The enclosed disk contains files to upgrade your TheraScribe® 3.0 or 3.5 program to include the behavioral definitions, goals, objectives, interventions, and diagnoses from *The Gay and Lesbian Treatment Planner.*

Note: You must have TheraScribe® 3.0 or 3.5 for Windows installed on your computer to use *The Gay and Lesbian Treatment Planner* library module.

To install the library module, please follow these steps:

1. Place the library module disk in your floppy drive.
2. Log in to TheraScribe® 3.0 or 3.5 as the Administrator using the name "Admin" and your administrator password.
3. On the Main Menu, press the "GoTo" button, and choose the Options menu item.
4. Press the "Import Library" button.
5. On the Import Library Module screen, choose your floppy disk drive a:\ from the list and press "Go." Note: It may take a few minutes to import the data from the floppy disk to your computer's hard disk.
6. When the installation is complete, the library module data will be available in your TheraScribe® 3.0 or 3.5 program.

---

*Note: This section applies only to the book with disk edition, ISBN 0-471-35081-8.

Note: If you have a network version of TheraScribe® 3.0 or 3.5 installed, you should import the library module one time only. After importing the data, the library module data will be available to all network users.

USER ASSISTANCE

If you need assistance using this TheraScribe® 3.0 or 3.5 add-on module, contact Wiley Technical Support at:

Phone: 212-850-6753
Fax: 212-850-6800 (Attention: Wiley Technical Support)
E-mail: techhelp@wiley.com

For information on how to install disk, refer to the **About the Disk** section on page 214.

WILEY

Publishers Since 1807